BACK ROADS THROUGH MIDDLE ENGLAND

BACK ROADS THROUGH MIDDLE ENGLAND

From Dorset to the Humber along the Jurassic stone belt

ANDREW BIBBY

Photographs by
John Morrison

GRITSTONE
PUBLISHING

Published in 2017 by
Gritstone Publishing Co-operative Ltd,
Birchcliffe Centre,
Hebden Bridge HX7 8DG

Gritstone Publishing Co-operative is jointly owned by its members, some of Britain's best-regarded authors writing about the countryside and the outdoors. Look out for our other titles. http://gritstone.coop

Cover photograph and photographs between pages 70 and 71 © John Morrison
Back cover illustration © Mike Bryson
Photograph on page 134 © the author

ISBN 978-0-9955609-3-2

Catalogue in publication data is available from the British Library

Printed in the UK by Imprint Digital, Exeter

Contents

Introduction

There had been no traffic for miles. The road was single track, and the only sound was that of bicycle wheels turning on tarmac. The countryside was gently wooded with fields and hedges, together with a distinct absence of houses or people. This was a back road that was going nowhere very much, and going there very slowly.

I knew I was cycling on a transport artery which had been a feature of the landscape for almost two thousand years. I was on the Fosse Way, the Roman road that made its way diagonally across the middle of England's countryside linking Lincoln with Leicester and the West Country. Most Roman roads in Britain led to London. The Fosse Way was the exception, the Roman equivalent as it were of a slow journey on Cross-Country Trains.

There are places today where the Fosse Way is a major highway, where cyclists have to take chances in sharing a road with heavy lorries and fast-moving cars. But I was cycling the very quietest part of the Fosse Way, the part which it seems almost nobody these days chooses to use. I was somewhere in west Wiltshire (or just possibly it was already the very southern tip of Gloucestershire) and I was enjoying myself making my way along the sort of tiny country lanes which earlier generations of cyclists may have taken for granted but which today seems most of the time a forgotten memory.

The carriageway became even narrower, and a temporary sign warned that the road ahead was blocked. The reason became apparent down the next hill, where a small stone bridge over a very small stream was in the process of being repaired. Cars would have had no chance but bicycles could just about squeeze through the roadworks. I had a cheery exchange with the two men from the county council who were going about their work in a suitably leisurely fashion. Only afterwards I thought that I should have asked if they'd come across any Roman stonework at the very foundations of the bridge. But perhaps the Roman legionnaires had splashed through the stream here in a ford. Perhaps the bridge the workmen were repairing had only been here for centuries, not millennia.

Beyond the bridge was a small hill and there at the top the first house for miles. It was set back a little from the road, built of honey-coloured stone and with a roof which was partly made of thatch. I cycled past before I realised I should have stopped to photograph it: a classic example of what everyone thinks of as the English country cottage. This was the sort of place to fuel back-to-the-country dreams of city dwellers. I felt I had stumbled across the English equivalent of what the French call *France profonde*: deep countryside, far from the normal busyness of life. Whoever lived here, you felt, was living about as far as you could get in England before the wheels of everyday life stopped turning altogether and time stood still.

Although rationally I knew that it wasn't really like that at all. The stone-and-thatch house beside the Fosse Way would be recorded in a whole bank of databases, just like every other home in Britain. It would be on the local authority records. There'd be council tax to pay, and in exchange the bins no doubt would regularly be put out and regularly emptied. There'd be a postcode. Direct mail companies would know the best sort of mailshots to send. The Land Registry would tell you who owned the house, if you felt like paying a few pounds to find out.

And indeed the people who lived there, when I looked at the map more closely later on, weren't really that far from things. The M4 was just a few miles north. You could probably commute to Swindon or Bath or Bristol. Possibly you could even commute to London if you had a comfortable car or didn't mind shelling out for a season ticket into Paddington.

Nowhere in England is undiscovered land, out of time, even if it just momentarily felt that way to me one Wednesday morning in September. I was making my way steadily northwards, choosing the very smallest tarmac roads I could find to carry me forward. When I reached this stretch of the Fosse Way I was on my third day of cycling, with another five to go before I would reach my journey's end. The plan was to cycle from the English Channel to the Humber. I had started at Burton Bradstock, a pleasant town on the west Dorset coast close to Bridport. My destination was to be Winteringham, a settlement up among the rushes on the southern side of the Humber estuary.

And the obvious question for you to ask me is, why? Why this route? It was the question my friends posed when I explained what I was planning. Why Dorset? Why north Lincolnshire? Land's End to John O'Groats they could have understood. Cycling coast-to-coast across northern England made sense. Even all the way on the Fosse Way itself could perhaps have been the basis of a journey.

But I do have an answer to this question: I had chosen to follow a geological line on the map. The Jurassic limestone which crosses England diagonally has had a direct effect on the landscape. It is responsible for the stone which has made the towns and villages of the Cotswolds so attractive to generations of visitors. It is responsible too for those could-almost-be-Cotswold villages in Dorset, and Somerset, and north Northamptonshire. Jurassic limestone has made towns and cities such as Bath, Oxford and Stamford. It has built Lincoln cathedral.

W.G. Hoskins, in his classic book *The Making of the English Landscape,* called this line of Jurassic limestone 'the great stone belt'.* I'm not sure whether the phrase was Hoskins' own coining or whether he was simply quoting others but either way the term is apposite and one which I am certainly happy to repeat – even if, looking at the map, it might be more accurate to describe this as England's shoulder strap rather than its belt.

The Jurassic stone provides us with what is often taken as the typical English scene, Hoskins said. He talked of the 'suave beauty' to be found, for example, in the limestone lands of Rutland. Yet my impression is that – apart perhaps from estate agents – England's great Jurassic stone belt is not really in most people's consciousness. I'm not sure that its effect on the English landscape from Dorset to the Humber is properly understood. My aim as I got myself and my bicycle ready for departure was to trace that geological line on the ground and see for myself what I could find.

How do you know where the limestone runs? It's surprisingly easy. You go online to the British Geological Survey website, where the BGS has helpfully made all its detailed geological maps of the country publicly and freely available. Adjust the map scale so that the information is neither too detailed or too generic, and there snaking its way across your computer screen can be seen the dark cream and the light cream bands that mark what Hoskins referred to collectively as 'cotswoldstone' and what we should more properly describe as the Great Oolite and Inferior Oolite limestone.

With the BGS website on the computer screen in front of me, I found an ordinary UK road atlas, pulled out a stubby pencil and slowly began tracing a thick pencil line from village to village and town to town across the country, following as closely as I could manage those cream bands on the BGS map. When I had finished – when the pencil had arrived at the Humber – I had my route. Some people would no doubt say that cyclists need a proper handlebar-mounted GPS device, but I found the road atlas

* Details of books and sources of information used in this work can be found at the end of the book.

ideal for picking out the tiny white back roads which I was keen to discover. After that, the preparation consisted of straightforwardly chopping up the atlas (it was an old one) into convenient pieces which would go in a plastic bag on top of my handlebar bag. As I'd find out as the journey unrolled, there would be significant satisfaction every forty or fifty miles in reaching the top of one map sheet and starting again at the bottom of the next.

It was William Smith, the man who has been given the accolade of 'the father of English geology', who first drew a band on a map across southern and mid-England to mark the line of the Jurassic limestone. He was the first to come up with the concept of producing geological maps, coloured according to the underlying rock formations, and the British Geological Survey's online version today is the direct descendant of his pioneering efforts (Smith chose cream for the Jurassic limestone for his map, too).

Smith chose to name this limestone as 'oolite', creating the word from the Greek for egg. Smith wanted to describe the fact that the limestone appears to be full of tiny little eggs, rather like an endless stream of tiny frog spawn or fish roe. There are two main oolitic strata in Britain and they were laid down at different times during the Jurassic geological period. First came the Inferior Oolite, inferior only in the sense that it is found underneath the later Great Oolite. Sandwiched between them, representing very many millions of intervening years of geology, are other rock and clay deposits, most notably Fuller's Earth, and yet despite this time gap the Great Oolite and Inferior Oolite strata follow each other closely across the BGS map and across the English countryside.

My first plan as I poised my pencil over the atlas was to stick as far as possible just to the band of Great Oolite. I wanted to give a certain discipline to my venture, so that I wasn't tempted to deviate too far off route. The Great Oolite would get me – broadly speaking – satisfactorily from Dorset through Somerset and the Cotswolds, into Oxfordshire and up through Northamptonshire to southern Lincolnshire. But the Great Oolite more or less peters out north of Lincoln. Some flexibility was needed. Geological maps are complicated. Rock strata are not necessarily neat and tidy affairs. As long my cycle route followed the great stone belt, whatever the precise geology, I told myself that I would be on course. And Winteringham was to be the final destination, I decided. It is true that the rocks north of the Humber are from the Jurassic period, too, and indeed that a tiny sliver of Inferior Oolite can be found for a few miles in east Yorkshire but I decided not to notice that. From coast to coast – or at least from coast to estuary: that was to be my journey.

This is not a book primarily about geology, however, or for that matter about my cycle journey. My intention is different. This is a book about particular English landscapes, and my aim is to try to comprehend those landscapes better, to get beyond the superficial to discover why the land looks the way it does. Landscape, let's remember, is what you get from human interaction with the land itself. Landscape is a dynamic concept, changing as human engagement with, and use of, the land changes.

So to try to get to grips with the English countryside along the great stone belt I found myself having to make a second journey, a desk-based one, to complement my bike ride. This involved me delving into a range of issues and subjects and disciplines which perhaps aren't necessarily normally covered in travel books. I wanted to find out more, for example, about the history of the way this land has been used, and the alternative visions which humans have had over the years as to how it could be used better. I knew I needed to understand the economics of the countryside better, and that meant understanding the important – and changing – role played by agriculture. I found myself looking at social matters, such as how and where we are choosing to build new homes in the countryside and what we are doing to try to maintain our rural communities. I gingerly took some steps into contentious country, such as how the land is actually owned.

As you'll find out, this, my second journey of discovery, also included arranging to talk to a wide range of people living along the great stone belt. They were people who in very different ways were having a direct engagement with the land and the landscape and who would, I felt, have insights to share. I'm grateful for the efforts they took in responding to my questions.

I have called this book *Back Roads through Middle England*, and perhaps I need to offer an explanation. Middle England is one of those terms which has slipped into British journalism in recent years, perhaps borrowed from the comparable term from across the Atlantic, Middle America. It is, I think, often given a slightly pejorative ring by journalists. Middle England is not a geographical place (it's certainly not synonymous with the Midlands) but from a London perspective it is definitely on the wrong side of the M25. Middle England, you feel, is a place out of touch with the artistic, intellectual and social buzz of metropolitan life. It's probably a place of sleepy conformity, almost certainly of unthinking nimbyism and quite possibly of political prejudice. Middle England is locked in the past, at a time when the country needs to engage with the present.

But my Middle England turns out to be an altogether more complicated, and more contested, terrain. Middle England is not a place of homogeneity, it is where people live and work and argue, a place where things change and don't change, where some are inspired with a hope to make their lives and their communities different but where others hold contrary viewpoints and follow other paths. It is the interplay between all these human efforts over the centuries which has provided the dynamic drive which has shaped the English landscape we know today.

The English countryside along the great stone belt is, of course, a beautiful place, one to cherish and enjoy. But it's even more rewarding, I'd suggest, when we have learned the language of the landscape. When we can understand what the countryside is telling us.

Burton Bradstock

The English Channel wasn't looking very inviting. The sea was a nondescript grey sort of colour, and so was the sky. There was a little drizzle. Burton Bradstock's beach had a few dog walkers hurrying past but otherwise it was empty. I could have started my journey with a ritualistic dipping of my toes in the sea, but I really wasn't tempted. Wet toes and damp sand inside my cycling shoes? – not a good idea. I looked instead up at the café just above the beach.

The main settlement of Burton Bradstock is a little way inland, tucked into a sheltered little valley in the lee of the cliffs. To get to the sea I had to cycle eastwards almost out of the village before turning across the traffic into the encouragingly named Beach Road. A small development of modern suburban houses (not a single one of them glowing with the warmth of Jurassic stone, I noticed with disappointment) takes you down to a grassy hillside which is almost entirely given over to car parking. In the season, this beach must be heaving and the National Trust raking in the parking fees. I was there when the car park was almost as empty as the beach.

But the café was open. I ordered two americanos, one for me and one for the person whom I had persuaded to come and meet me. We found a quiet corner where we could talk, and I pulled out my notebook.

My guest was Professor Denys Brunsden, one of the key players in the small team of people who managed to persuade UNESCO that the coastline here was so special that it deserved having World Heritage status. He is now retired, living a short distance away on the Dorset/Devon border, his academic achievements recognised in his status as an Emeritus Professor at King's College, London. He has held a string of eminent posts, including the President of the Geographical Association and the first President of the International Association of Geomorphologists, and he also has an OBE, awarded for services to conservation as well as for his academic achievements. The eastern Devon and Dorset coast is the part of the world which he has studied more closely during his career than anywhere else so if anyone could explain to me why this coastline was quite so interesting I reckoned it would be him.

The signs welcoming visitors to the Jurassic Coast have now been up for several years, and what we could perhaps call world heritage tourism is important hereabouts. The Dorset and East Devon Coast was in fact officially inscribed into UNESCO's list of World Heritage sites in December 2001, but of course that was simply the culmination of a long process of planning, campaigning and detailed report writing. The story begins at least ten years earlier. Denys Brunsden recalls how, almost as an aside at the end of a talk he was giving in the early 1990s at a local event, he commented on the significance of the area. "I said, 'This is a fantastic coast. It's the sort of area which could be a world heritage site'. There were two planning officers from Dorset and Devon county councils sitting at the back of the meeting and I saw them muttering to each other. Afterwards they came up to me and asked me: 'Did you really mean it?'," he says. An idea had begun to take root.

Quite rightly it takes a lot to convince UNESCO, the UN's Paris-based arm concerned with education, science and culture, that something is worthy of world heritage status. Britain has thirty-one world heritage sites, including Stonehenge, Hadrian's Wall, the Tower of London, industrial heritage centres such as Ironbridge Gorge, and cities such as Edinburgh and Bath. The Giant's Causeway in Northern Ireland is on the list as well, because of its geological importance. And thanks to the work of the small team of people who worked hard to make it happen, the Dorset and East Devon Coast is there too.

The official nomination document was drawn up by the two county councils with a great deal of input from an independent body of landowners, community bodies and agencies called the Dorset Coast Forum which Denys Brunsden chaired. Eventually, in 2000, the bid to UNESCO was ready for submission. It ran to over 250 pages, but fortunately Denys Brunsden was prepared to offer me a quick digest. The first reason why this coastline is important, he explained, is because it provides a nearly continuous set of rock formations illustrating around 185 million years of the history of the Earth.

The World Heritage site itself stretches from Orcombe Rocks near Exmouth to Studland Bay on the edge of Poole Harbour in Dorset, with the oldest rocks being at the western end. Take a walk from Exmouth to

Studland and, as the miles go by, the rocks gradually become younger. Indeed, you will be beginning your walk as it were around 250 Ma (million years ago) and will end your journey around 66 Ma. "A walk along the shore is a walk through time," Denys Brunsden told me. "The layers of rock go under, with younger rocks on top – it's the classic geological principle of succession."

If that was the first argument made to UNESCO in the 'statement of significance' in the submission document, there was also a second convincing case to be made too. The story of this stretch of coastline has been intimately connected with the history of the growing human understanding of the science of geology. Early pioneering scientists came down to this part of the south coast to explore for themselves what the rocks and geological formations could tell them.

One of these visitors was William Smith, whom I introduced briefly in the last chapter as the man who had named the Jurassic oolite limestone which my bicycle and I were now about to follow. Smith's story is deservedly well known. The son of a blacksmith, Smith was born in a Cotswold village in 1769 and brought up by his uncle when his father died young. Despite being largely self-educated Smith was clearly intelligent, and he was also observant. He started working in 1787 as an assistant to a local surveyor and then a few years later began undertaking work on his own account. This took him south to the Somerset coal fields where he was engaged for eight years in surveying work in preparation for the construction of the Somerset coal canal, being built to take the coal from the mines to market. This work involved naturally enough examining and assessing the rocks through which the canal would be built, and Smith made a discovery. He noticed that the rocks were arranged in layers, or strata, with the rock beds dipping down gradually in an easterly direction, and that the same basic arrangement of the different layers of rocks could be found in different locations. There appeared to be a consistent relationship between the strata, in other words, even if the same rocks were to be found at different depths below the surface.

This was a breakthrough in English geological understanding, and led to him being given the nickname by some of William 'Strata' Smith. "For six years I put my notions of stratification to the test of excavation; and I generally pointed out to contractors and others, who came to undertake the work, what the various parts of the canal would be dug through," he later wrote. Nevertheless there remained the problem that one layer of rock could at first glance look remarkably like another: "the great similarity of the rocks of the Oolite, on and near the end of the canal towards Bath, required more than superficial observation," he explained. His solution was a remarkable one. He noticed that that the rocks contained fossils, and in collecting the fossils he realised that each different stratum contained their own distinctive types of fossil. You could reliably identify the different rock strata by the fossils they contained.

William Smith, who was later to travel the country putting this theory of his to the test, had been down on the Dorset and Devon coast mapping the geology near Charmouth around 1795 and he returned again to Weymouth in 1812. Other famous names in early English geology came to this part of the coast too: Adam Sedgwick (the man who was to give Smith the title of the 'father' of English geology), William Buckland, William Conybeare, Roderick Murchison and many others. This coast, to quote the submission which went to UNESCO, "has been a crucible of earth science investigations" for very many years.

My americano was getting cold as my notebook filled up. Denys Brunsden had moved on from geology to palaeontology, and was describing the extraordinary richness of the fossils to be found along the coast. The key historical figure this time was a woman, Mary Anning, a local working-class woman from Lyme Regis with little formal education who nevertheless was to become arguably the greatest fossil collector of them all. Anning, who was born in 1799, earned her living by selling the fossils which she discovered and then painstakingly unearthed along the west Dorset shoreline. With other members of her family she found the first fossil of an ichthyosaur (a large marine reptile) to come to scientific attention, the world's first complete plesiosaur (another marine reptile which is also extinct unless, that is, the Loch Ness Monster really does exist) and the first British pterodactyl. She also made equally important if less dramatic discoveries of fossils of invertebrates.

The shoreline along this part of the South Coast remains a rich source of fossils, and if visitors naturally tend to think of dinosaur bones and fossilised footprints, perhaps the really characteristic fossil is the ammonite, the familiar spiral shape which marks where a mollusc once lived. Ammonites vary depending on the age of the rock, and therefore make an excellent 'index fossil' – an identifier of individual rock strata.

For much of the Jurassic period what is now Devon and Dorset (and indeed much of southern England and the east Midlands) was a subtropical shallow sea, and the fossils are the records of the variety of marine reptiles, fish, molluscs and mammals who lived their lives here. The tiny 'eggs' of the oolite limestone are the fossilised remains of grains of sand and fragments of shell which were rolled around on the shallow sea floor. But the changing variations in the fossils, and the changing nature of the rock strata themselves which make up the geological record of the Jurassic period (since the Great and Inferior Oolite are simply two strata among many, including other limestones, sandstones, mudstones and clays) remind us of just what an enormously long stretch of time geological time embraces. The Jurassic period alone extends over hundreds of millions of years.

So perhaps the ten years or so taken to work up the UNESCO application wasn't really so long after all. The original plan, I was told, had been to bid for the coastline all the way from Torquay to Studland but in the end it was decided to focus simply on the area east of Exmouth. All the landowners along the coastline had to be engaged and won over, and thanks mainly to detailed preparatory work only one of the 480 individual landowners in the end raised an objection. In 2001, Denys Brunsden, together with his colleague Tim Badman who had prepared the key documentation, went across to Helsinki, to the meeting of UNESCO's World Heritage committee, to learn their fate. It sounds as if the evening afterwards was a pretty cheerful occasion.

The Dorset and East Devon Coast – technically just the narrow 155 km-long strip of land between the cliff top and the low-water mark – was duly inscribed as a World Heritage site. But the full title, Denys Brunsden and his colleagues knew, was clumsy and rather uninspiring. It was another key member of the original team, Malcolm Turnbull, who came up with the popular name. He'd already coined the term Jurassic Coast for an earlier project looking at geo-tourism along the Dorset coast. Why not use the term for the World Heritage site as well, he suggested?

Let's be honest. There is a little geological sleight of hand going on here. It's true that the bulk of the geology of the Dorset coastline is Jurassic, or in other words dating from 200 Ma to 145 Ma. But the western section in Devon is pre-Jurassic, the period which geologists call the Triassic (251 Ma – 200 Ma). Meanwhile the rocks in the furthest eastern parts of the coast, into Purbeck and round the chalk stacks of Old Harry Rocks to Studland, are later, belonging to the Cretaceous period. There is a single geological name for these three periods taken together, and it is the Mesozoic. Really, the tourist signs should be pointing you to the Mesozoic coast.

Yes, we had problems with the name, Malcolm Turnbull admitted to me when I was to meet him later at his house in Swanage. Yes, we could have called it the Mesozoic Coast, he went on. "But who has heard of Mesozoic? Whereas everyone has heard of the Jurassic, because of Jurassic Park," he added. Jurassic means dinosaurs. Jurassic is, put bluntly, a strong marketing brand. And the Jurassic Coast is what the tourists want to visit.

And the point is that the geological heritage from hundreds of millions of years past is now having a direct effect on this part of England today. "The effect of world heritage status brings millions of pounds into the economy," Malcolm Turnbull told me. "I've seen tourism change. The bucket and spade tourism of the 1960s and 1970s is dropping off, and now we're getting lots of visitors coming at other times of the year, in March and April and October for example."

Geology may provide the foundations but it is human engagement with the land which creates landscapes. Tourism is a significant factor hereabouts, so tourism too plays its part in shaping the way that communities develop and buildings and land are utilised. Tourism celebrates the landscape, but at the same time it also subtly changes the landscape.

Around me at Burton Bradstock I could identify this for myself. Over *there* was the carefully landscaped car parking, *there* the interpretation board on the beach, *there* the engineered coastal path heading up to the cliffs. And here was the most obvious addition to the Burton Bradstock beach landscape: my welcoming beach café. The coffee was cold and the interview was over. I said good-bye to Denys Brunsden with a handshake and he returned to his car.

Burton Bradstock was just the start of my journey, however. My way ran northwards.

Powerstock

I stopped that first morning in the market town of Beaminster. There was a café at the back of one of the shops overlooking the small market square. Cake may have been involved as well. Carb loading, we cyclists call it.

I hadn't been to Beaminster before. It is, let's be frank, not really somewhere you stumble upon by accident. But I did know of the town by literary reputation.

Perhaps that's putting it just a little strongly. Beaminster is the theme of one of the poems written in Dorset dialect by the nineteenth century poet William Barnes. This is how his poem starts:

Sweet Be'mi'ster, that bist a-bound
By green an' woody hills all round,
Wi' hedges reachen up between
A thousan' vields o' zummer green,
Where elems' lofty heads do drow
Their sheädes vor haÿ-meäkers below,
An' wild hedge-flow'rs do charm the souls
O' maïdens in their evenen strolls.

William Barnes is still remembered today in Dorset, as – if you want to put it this way – the county's national poet. In fact, recent years have begun to see the institution of William Barnes celebrations held on 7 October, the date on which he died in 1886. What began as something of a throw-away idea in a newspaper (if the Scots can have Burns Night, why can't we have a Barnes Night?) seems to be gaining traction. If I'd arranged my cycle ride differently I might have been able to join the Wessex Morris Men in the Barnes Night bash they were organising.

The use of dialect in poetry such as William Barnes's work may raise some eyebrows. Can it be treated, for example, as 'serious' literature or is it merely to be seen as some sort of whimsy or a novelty act? I hope that there are few people these days who would want to maintain the argument that regional dialect is inherently inferior to standard English (after all, as has been pointed out, we all speak dialect of one kind or another, even those of us for whom our dialect is RP). Nevertheless at the time when Barnes was writing, Dorset dialect would certainly have been looked down on by many of his contemporaries. For that matter, it still can be. Fake West Country 'mummerset' accents continue to be thought of as something to be laughed at. Stick a battered straw hat on your head and chew on a piece of grass to complete the comic effect.

But William Barnes was not playing this game. His intention, he wrote in the introduction to his first book of poems published in 1844, was "not to show up the simplicity of rural life as an object of sport". He wanted to use dialect for another reason: perhaps because he felt that this was the language which best helped him write about the Dorset landscape and the lives of those who lived in it.

Barnes's poems have been wrongly described as peasant poetry. In fact he was never an agricultural labourer (his family and relatives mostly came from a tenant farming background) and he himself was well educated, a man who taught himself Latin and Greek and then worked as a school-master in a series of schools which he established and ran. Later, when he was in his forties, he started working for a degree in Divinity from Cambridge University getting his degree through what we would now call distance learning. He also became ordained as an Anglican cleric.

But he had an unerring ear for local speech rhythms and language, picked up he says from "the associations of an early youth that was passed among rural families of a secluded part of the county".

William Barnes had every right to write his poems in Dorset tongue and certainly his work has been appreciated by those who should know: Tennyson reportedly admired his verse, Thomas Hardy edited a selection of his poetry, and my more recent edition of the poems also includes a very positive quote from W.H. Auden. But you can question whether there is much more to be found in the poetry beyond Barnes's pastoralism and his gently nostalgic tone for better days long past. Sometimes in Barnes it feels as though this is the Dorset countryside being interpreted and served up to meet the expectations of an urban readership.

But I type this last sentence with caution: I'm conscious that this is an ever-present risk which can affect all of us who undertake to write about landscape.

Beaminster has remained three-syllabic since Barnes's day (although today it is pronounced 'bem-minster' rather than 'bem-mister') and something else is the same, too. Have another look at those first two lines of Barnes's poem again. Sweet Beaminster is surrounded by hills all round. Indeed it is. That first morning's cycle ride produced the steepest, meanest hill climbs of my whole journey. And the worst climb by a very long way was the climb a few miles south of Beaminster, as I left the village of Powerstock.

Partly I only had myself to blame. I had chosen the very back roads (the ones that tend to be the hilliest) out from Burton Bradstock mainly because I was keen to include Powerstock on my route.

Powerstock is even less likely to be stumbled on by accident than Beaminster. It straggles up the side of a hill, its church and many of its houses showing off what can be done with the Dorset version of Jurassic limestone. There's a pub and a primary school but no village shop. Its small branch line railway station is long closed. And there's potentially another absence in the village, if you're looking for somewhere to live.

This was why I had arranged to meet Vanessa White at her house down the lane near the pub. Vanessa retired recently from a senior management post in the health service in west Dorset and now chairs the Powerstock and District Community Land Trust, a local voluntary organisation that has been working hard over recent years to bring a clutch of new affordable homes to a patch of scrubland in the village. It sounds initially unlikely: isn't every villager in Middle England concerned to keep new housing developments out of their backyard? How could it be that in Powerstock there's a community group trying to do just the opposite?

We've been in Powerstock for over thirty years, Vanessa tells me, and the village has changed. "When we came there was only one holiday cottage," she explains. Now around one in three are holiday cottages and that takes its toll on community life. "We didn't want to be just a holiday village. Powerstock has always been a working village, a living village and we didn't want to see that changing," she adds.

So when a housing officer from the local district council set up a meeting to see if there was any interest in a community-led initiative to create affordable housing in Powerstock she got involved. "We said 'OK, let's explore the idea'." A committee took shape, and the work started. That was about five years ago. Now, many months on, the land has been identified, the plans are drawn up and the freehold transfer of the site for the houses is about to go through. Very shortly the first residents will be making their homes in the eight new houses that the trust is putting up.

It would be inaccurate to imply that there was no opposition to the idea. Of course there was. But nevertheless the Powerstock Community Land Trust, which is working on the development in conjunction with a local housing association, has clearly managed to get most of the village behind its project. "We held a straw poll at the public meeting where we first took the decision to go through the planning process. There were about eighty people there, and 63 were in favour and three against," Vanessa says. "But it's taken us a long time," she adds.

Like many English villages, Powerstock has a local landowner estate down the road which owns much of the farmland and many of the cottages. The estate was sold privately in the 1930s and many of the houses which were kept originally to be rented to estate workers were sold on the open market. The current owner of the estate, conscious of the effect this has had on the village, has stopped the sales and has also agreed to pass the land for the new homes across to the trust for a nominal £1. But there are still the solicitors' fees to be paid to sort out the switch in ownership. And there are also all the challenges of progressing the plans through the planning process. "We're a conservation area, and in an Area of Outstanding Natural Beauty," Vanessa explains. The council's conservation officers had particular demands, and then there were tree preservation orders to address. The site was also identified as potentially a habitat for dormice and slowworms. "You need to be prepared to be patient," is how Vanessa puts it.

Who are the new homes for? The answer is that they are for people who are either already living in the community, have family connections to Powerstock and its neighbourhood or who work in the village or nearby. They have to have had a local connection for several years and be on the district council housing register, I'm told. Take the case of the daughter and her partner who are currently living with her parents in an ex-council house in the village but need a place of their own. Or the couple who are getting on in years and need to move down from their isolated house as they get older. Vanessa White is sure of one thing: the houses will find ready tenants.

"It's very rewarding. People thought we couldn't do it, but we have, we're able to give something back to the community," Vanessa says. And it turns out that Powerstock and District Community Land Trust is by no means unusual in what it's doing. Across the West Country, in villages with names like Worth Matravers, Toller Porcorum, Yarlington and Norton-sub-Hamdon, CLTs have successfully completed small but locally important affordable housing projects. Community Land Trusts are also a feature of other parts of the country, including in inner-city areas such as Anfield in Liverpool. There are, I gathered, approaching 200 CLTs nationwide. This is a movement that is growing.

And after the eight new houses in Powerstock are built? What next? "People are already saying, 'What we need next, Vanessa, is sheltered accommodation for the elderly'," Vanessa White says, adding that, if the future of the village pub was ever to be in doubt, this could be another project for the CLT. Other CLTs elsewhere have certainly diversified beyond housing.

Once, when transport was slow and laborious, rural settlements housed those who worked in the local economy, predominantly in agriculture. Today, travel between city and country is hardly an issue, and the link between living in a village and working there has been fractured. (Most of Powerstock's holiday homes are owned by Londoners, I was told: with a little help from the M3 and M27 you can get down in under three hours.) But what does this mean for community life?

English villages, like the landscape itself, have over the centuries been places of change but today that's perhaps less true. These days it can seem as though the desire is there to keep everything just as it is: change (including new homes to help keep local people in their own communities) is challenging.

So I found what was happening in Powerstock inspiring, almost enough to fortify me for the hill which was waiting to greet me up beyond the church. And I knew that if I really wanted to get to grips with the landscape in this part of England I needed to tackle the very issue which Vanessa White and her colleagues in Powerstock were indirectly addressing.

My cycle ride took me through a string of beautiful villages like Powerstock, past stone-built houses and cottages like that one I had glimpsed from the Fosse Way, and as I cycled I found myself mulling over some questions. Who are our villages for? Who should live in them? Should we look to build new houses? Should we fight to keep the land untouched?

Odcombe

In hindsight, I should probably be embarrassed that the first day's cycling only took me to the outskirts of Yeovil. But on something of a whim I had decided that I wanted to stay in the village of Odcombe. The local pub had a lawn at the back which was given over to camping. It seemed an ideal arrangement.

So I took my time. I stopped off for something to eat at the village shop in Halstock, which as the signs proudly told me is now owned and run by the community. There's a meeting room there where they let me sit down to eat the sandwiches I'd bought. And I stopped too at the attractive little village of East Coker where I visited the church. ·

East Coker has, it has to be said, a somewhat greater relationship to English poetry than William Barnes's Beaminster. T.S. Eliot gave the village's name to the second of his *Four Quartets*, meditations on human existence, religious faith and the nature of time which were written over a six year period just before and during the Second World War. Eliot had visited the village of East Coker in the summer of 1939, about the time he began writing *East Coker* the poem. Eliot was American by birth, being born in 1888 in St Louis, although he lived much of his adult life in Britain and became a British subject. It was in East Coker, Eliot discovered, that some of his English ancestors had lived and it was in East Coker church that Eliot later decided he wanted his ashes to be buried after his death. The church, a fine building primarily of the fifteenth century, has a small memorial plaque to the poet near the altar.

By the time he wrote *East Coker* Eliot had embraced a high-church Anglicanism (George Orwell once criticised the 'melancholy faith' which, he felt, had led to the 'gloomy mumblings' of the *Four Quartets*; Orwell preferred Eliot's earlier work). Eliot had by this stage also embraced a conservative approach to English history, which perhaps can be sensed in the mood and tone which imbue *East Coker*.

At East Coker I found myself in a village which had taken a very different approach to the housing issue from the one I had discovered in Powerstock. Just a short time before, local people had been up in arms about plans for a major new housing development, part of it to be within East Coker's parish boundary. There were, according to the local paper, 'Impassioned pleas to save the village immortalised by poet T.S. Eliot'. The T.S. Eliot Society in the United States had weighed in, opposing anything that would destroy the beauty of the village. There was talk of East Coker being 'swamped' by urban expansion.

But the planning authority, South Somerset District Council, had held to its original plan and the objectors had withdrawn, defeated. The background to all this was the preparation of the Local Plan, the document which local authorities are required to produce to give a long-term strategic programme within which development can be planned. Next-door Yeovil would need to grow over the next fifteen years or so, and the obvious area for it to grow – the planners proposed – was out to the south of the town centre. 1500 or so houses were scheduled to be built there in the years up to 2028, with a further thousand or so thereafter.

The heart of East Coker village is a delightful place, with many of the buildings built of the local Hamstone Jurassic limestone from nearby Ham Hill. I pictured the village devastated by new suburban housing. Then, later on, I looked at the maps in the Local Plan for myself and thought the protestors might have been overstating their case. The new proposed area of housing is indeed partly in East Coker parish but it is a considerable distance north of East Coker's historic heart, much closer to the neighbouring settlement of North Coker and separated from there by a buffer of remaining countryside.

Planning always seems to be controversial, although what we have is clearly better than the free-for-all which would exist if there were no planning frameworks or strategic plans at all. But planning involves sometimes highly significant changes to the land. People need homes. People also have a deep attachment to the landscapes of their neighbourhoods. Sometimes strategic planning can be difficult work.

I cycled up the small hill away from East Coker church and made my way for a few miles round the western edge of Yeovil. I cycled through an industrial area and past a large Asda which the map told me was in an area called Preston Plucknett. There I picked up a quiet back road which led me to the village of Odcombe and the village pub.

The reason why I had thought of visiting Odcombe was a song dating back to the nineteenth century which many years before I had stumbled across in a collection of ballads and folk songs. The song was entitled *Come all you bold fellows that follow the plough*. Here's the verse where Odcombe gets a mention, along with Preston Plucknett and several other neighbouring villages:

> From Langport and Martock we'll meet at Stoke Cross
> For the fat-bellied farmers we don't care a toss,
> From Odcombe and Preston and Montacute too
> We'll come with flags flying and ribbons of blue.

Who were the 'we', and why the flags and ribbons? The song, which dates from the early 1870s, turns out to be describing one of the rallies held by local agricultural labourers in this part of Somerset in an attempt to improve their lot in life by forming an agricultural trade union. Here's how the song starts:

> Come all you bold fellows that follow the plough,
> Either hedging or ditching or milking the cow;
> The time has arrived and the Union flag waves:
> We won't be kept down like a lot of white slaves.

The agricultural labourer has almost disappeared from our collective sense of English history. Yet in relatively recent times the countryside was chock-full of families who (as the song said) hedged, ditched and milked cows as well as doing all the other tasks necessary to keep the fields producing the food which a growing urban population needed. In the middle of the nineteenth century – in the census of 1851, to be absolutely precise – there were one and a half million people in Britain who described themselves as agricultural labourers, shepherds, farm servants or something similar.

Their role in the making of the English countryside was considerable, but their contribution is easily overlooked. The historian Eric Hobsbawm once put it this way: "The marvellous surface of the British landscape, the work of their ploughs, spades and shears and the beasts they looked after, bears no signature or mark such as the masons left on cathedrals". With few exceptions, agricultural labourers were in no position to tell their own story for the benefit of posterity.

Agricultural labourers weren't farmers. They worked for farmers as hired hands, sometimes in more or less permanent jobs but sometimes in seasonal or very temporary work. Farmers (most were tenant-farmers) were members of a separate, higher, social class. In turn, above the farmers were the landowners, including the great landowning aristocratic families with giant estates in different areas of the country. If there had ever in the past been a sense of paternalistic social obligation towards those who occupied lower rungs of the social ladder in the countryside (and be warned that this reading of history is itself contested), such an approach was certainly firmly on the way out by the nineteenth century. Increasingly (particularly following the abolition of protectionism on home grown grain with the repeal of the corn laws in 1846) agriculture became driven by market forces.

Agricultural labourers were dirt poor. Indeed, perhaps we have allowed ourselves to forget this part of our national history in order to save ourselves the embarrassment we might otherwise still be feeling. The use of the term 'white slaves' of the song might seem excessive to us today, but the facts speak of people caught in desperate servitude. A labourer in the fields around the time of the early 1870s would have earned about twelve shillings a week (there were twenty shillings to the pound). Wages were particularly low in the south of England, and – most notably – in the West Country. We know from a Royal Commission that in Dorset, for example, labourers were typically being paid eight shillings a week at this time. Wives of labourers were also expected to work, as part of the deal struck between farmer and hired hand. Women undertook work such as weeding, manure spreading and stone picking, and would get a few pence a day.

Children, too, had to supplement the household income. Here is how one Somerset man, born in 1826 in Montacute just north of Odcombe, remembered his childhood: "I had to go to work at 5 years old for sixpence a week with scarce any clothes, only what my mother could beg from other people for me. I was sent at this early age to keep away rooks from the seed corn. I had to trudge about the fields from dawn to dark in all weathers, going to my work in summer as early as four o'clock in the morning with nothing but a morsel of bread for my breakfast.

"I continued year after year in this wretched slavery subject to the greatest harshness and cruelty. My master used to thrash me unmercifully whenever he was offended with himself or anyone else or nothing at all… The savage cruelty and brutality of the farmers, and of course, the men also, which I have seen practised towards poor little boys and girls who were sent out to work in the fields entirely beggars all description."

Home life was equally desperate. "The whole family were obliged to make the utmost exertions to get food to eat… Our food consisted principally of a little barley-cake, potatoes and salt, tea kettle broth and barley 'flippet' [barley meal in water]… Now and then I got what we used to call a hot dinner, that is to say, a piece of bread and an onion, at others a bit of bread and hard skim-cheese – so hard I had to soak it in water before I could eat it."

And sometimes there wasn't even this fare to be had: "When I got home at night, I many times found my father and mother so irritable from privation, that they would send me to bed without my supper as a pretended punishment, when, in reality, they had no food for me."

These were the reminiscences of childhood written down by a man called George Mitchell. Mitchell was unusual in that he successfully escaped the poverty of his upbringing. He describes the day when he realised that his future would have to lie outside Montacute: he was nineteen, still only on four shillings a week, and had already worked for eighteen hours when he found himself being verbally abused by his master for not being prepared to unload an additional waggon of hay. "I trudged home down Hollow Lane, resolving to bear that kind of life no more," he wrote. He moved to the stone quarries at nearby Ham Hill, learned the trade of stonemason and eventually moved to London where he built up a highly successful stonemason's business and became for a time a wealthy man.

We might feel that we have to ask whether Mitchell over-egged his account of the awfulness of his childhood in order to demonstrate the success he had made of his life. Yet there are very similar accounts of the lives of men, women and children in the countryside which bear out Mitchell's own account. The author and civil servant Francis George Heath visited Montacute in the 1870s as part of his research for a book and found there what he described as 'scenes of wretchedness': "Of all the distressing sights which one can witness anywhere, I do not know of anything that is more heart-rending than to see poor little children actually wanting [lacking] bread," he wrote. A string of Parliamentary and Royal Commission reports into labour conditions in agriculture, dating from the 1860s through to the 1880s, provide the data to collaborate Mitchell's and Heath's accounts.

How could the plight of agricultural labourers have been ignored? In part because they were treated as somehow not deserving of better. For much of this period they were known collectively as 'Hodge', a name which was usually used in a pejorative way (rather in the way that 'Paddy' was a convenient derogatory term to describe Irish people). There was, it could be suggested, something almost of the farmyard animal about Hodge as he 'chewed the cud'. He was, one writer put it, 'unimaginative, ill-clothed, ill-educated, ill-paid, ignorant of all that is taking place beyond his own village'.

Of course, the efforts forty years earlier by the group of agricultural workers in the Dorset village of Tolpuddle in 1833 to improve their lot collectively through a form of union is well known, and the story of their oppressive treatment by local landowning magistrates and their transportation to Australia has given the Tolpuddle Martyrs an honoured place in British trade union history. What had preceded the attempt by the men in Tolpuddle to organise in a formal self-help group had been a much more inchoate response by agricultural labourers to their plight. The years 1830 and 1831 had seen a wave of disturbances and rioting spread across much of the country areas in the south of England and Midlands, an episode which is normally referred to as the Swing Riots after the mysterious (and imaginary) character of 'Captain Swing' who sometimes put his name to the rioters' demands. Sporadic disturbances and episodes of arson continued in country areas in the years that followed, but if anything the plight of agricultural workers became even worse in the middle of the century. The potato blight of the 1840s which caused such suffering in Ireland also affected English agricultural workers. It was almost forty years after Tolpuddle before agricultural labourers turned once again to the idea of trade union organising.

In fact, it was in the year 1872 that the National Agricultural Labourers' Union first got under way, initially in Warwickshire under the leadership of the energetic (if sometimes somewhat egotistical) Joseph Arch. The area near Odcombe was one of the NALU's hot spots and the reason was because of the efforts of George Mitchell. Mitchell, living in London, threw himself into efforts to build a union branch in and around his home village and used his money to fund many of the costs incurred. It was he who organised a first meeting in Montacute on a day's holiday during Whitsun in June 1872, at which – so the local media reported – fifty-eight labourers enrolled as pioneering members of the union and paid the necessary sixpence deposit. Mitchell followed this up with other local recruitment events and a year later in 1873 began what was to be the first of an annual series of union rallies held nearby on Ham Hill, close to the site of an Iron Age hillfort. Joseph Arch was a speaker at several of these events.

I think we have to assume, therefore, that it was to Ham Hill that the parties from Odcombe, and Preston, and Montacute too, to say nothing of Langport and Martock, were making their way with their banners and ribbons in my song. Extraordinarily, a photograph of a Ham Hill rally (to be precise, the one held on Whit Monday in 1877) has survived. There, standing up addressing the crowd with his hands on his hips, is the figure of Joseph Arch. Sitting alongside Arch on the platform just below the hill brow can be seen George Mitchell himself, complete with a remarkably long and bushy beard.

The final verse of *Come all you bold fellows that follow the plough* is suitably upbeat:

All England will learn of our doings today,
As in grand procession we all march away;
And the down-trodden labourers will cry as they march
May God bless our hero, the brave Joseph Arch.

The rhyme would have been much more difficult to manage, but I have a sense that the real local hero who should have been celebrated in that last couplet was George Mitchell. I was embarrassed that I hadn't come across his name or knew the story behind the song when I arrived in Odcombe that afternoon, pitched the tent and retreated to the bar. I would perhaps have been even more embarrassed if I had read the contemporary press report of a speech given by Mitchell at one of the Montacute rallies where he had told his audience of a terrible sight he had seen that day in Odcombe: utterly impoverished children and a father who was drinking away his ten shillings wages a week – in the village pub.

The pub has changed, the village of Odcombe has changed, everything has changed since those days. Agriculture in Britain went into a period of prolonged economic depression in the later 1870s, partly the result of very cheap imported food arriving in Britain. The numbers of agricultural labourers fell rapidly as the twentieth century got under way, the result of a drift to the cities but also through mass emigration to countries such as New Zealand. Joseph Arch's union petered out in a few short years, as did the separate regional trade unions set up at the same time in other parts of the country. Mitchell continued organising (and funding) the Ham Hill rallies into the 1890s before eventually retreating to focus on his business and his family.

Mitchell had railed against the money sucked out of his community by the owner of the big house in the village ("Montacute House has not been regularly inhabited for forty years, and yet during that period nearly half a million of money has been extracted from this poverty-stricken district by one man, to be spent Heaven knows where"). Today the Elizabethan architectural masterpiece which is Montacute House is in the hands of the National Trust, open to the public in the summer and let out to be used by film companies for a host of period costume dramas. It is, deservedly, a highly popular visitor attraction. But I wonder how many visitors to the house stop by in the village of Montacute and look at the side of the stone drinking fountain there. It is here that a small brass plaque to the memory of George Mitchell was placed in 2001, a century after his death. Mitchell, I'd suggest, deserves greater fame than this. But at least not everyone in his home village has completely forgotten him.

Frome

I skirted round the north end of Yeovil the next morning, managing to pick up the little unclassified road north which I had spotted on my map. The villages passed: Adber, Corton Denham, Sutton Montis, South Cadbury. The road became hillier. South Cadbury abuts Cadbury Hill on which stands the impressive Bronze Age and Iron Age hill fort known as Cadbury Castle. For at least four hundred years local tradition has been that Cadbury Castle was the site of King Arthur's Camelot, a tradition based it would seem on almost no actual evidence at all apart, perhaps, from the fact that the river Cam (the Somerset version, not the Cambridgeshire one) runs nearby. Cadbury Castle is suitably evocative, though. People, whoever they were, did live their lives on this hilltop a very long time ago.

The community-run shop at North Cadbury provided a place for coffee, and then the villages resumed: Woolston, Yarlington, Shepton Montague, Redlynch, South Brewham. The destination for lunch was Frome, but Frome seemed a long time in coming. Frome nine miles, said a signpost. I cycled for what was surely several hours. Frome seven miles, said another sign. I began to remember that people have a phrase to describe a long way: a country mile. Signposts in this part of Somerset are definitely in country miles.

But Frome eventually arrived. This is a southern English town with an industrial, rather than purely agricultural, history and it shows in all sorts of ways. Wool was the cornerstone of the local economy for centuries, with woollen cloth being produced from the 1400s onwards, the industry expanding in the later seventeenth and early eighteenth centuries before going into a decline. By 1826, when William Cobbett came riding into the town on one of his journalistic forays which he later published as Rural Rides, the town's weavers were obviously in dire straits: "These poor creatures at Frome have pawned all their things, or nearly all. All of their best clothes, their blankets and sheets, their looms; any little piece of furniture that they had, and that was good for anything. Mothers have been compelled to pawn all the tolerably good clothes that their children had."

The workers' houses in the town, it seems, were a place of poverty at this time just as much as the agricultural labourers' cottages in the villages. Cobbett did find some people doing well in Frome, however, mostly those trading in all that "false paper stuff, called money". There were "swaggering fellows going about, with vulgarity imprinted upon their countenances, but with good clothes upon their backs," Cobbett complained.

This is vintage Cobbett, full of indignant outbursts at what he noticed on his travels. His object, as he wrote in the opening to the 1830 edition of Rural Rides was to 'see the country', and to do this properly, he argued, you had to seek out the by-lanes: you had to go either on foot or on horse-back. I'd like to think that he would have considered a bicycle a pretty good way of assessing the state of the country too.

My guide to twenty-first century Frome was to be a local town councillor, Peter Macfadyen, who met me in the back garden of a wholefoody-type café. "Frome has a history both of neglect and slightly bolshy independence," he told me. He is one of those in whom that spirit of bolshiness is currently most obviously being manifested.

Frome Town Council had been a pretty moribund affair, or so Peter claimed, until what he calls the bloodless revolution of 2011 took place. This was when a disparate group of community-minded activists came together under the Independents for Frome badge, and to many people's surprise won ten seats and took control. They promptly abolished the complicated traditional sub-committee structure of the council and replaced it with just two forums, one concerned with internal town council matters and one with external community affairs. The public were encouraged to come along and thrash out the issues.

Mainstream politicians tut-tutted, gave the new regime until Christmas that year and said it would end in tears. In fact, the Independents kept control, stood again in the elections four years later and this time swept the board, taking all seventeen seats.

Peter has come up with a clever name for what he and his colleagues are trying to institute in Frome: he calls it 'flatpack democracy'. It represents a move away from traditional representative politics and towards more directly participative D-I-Y democracy, and he argues that it is a way of bringing back energy into a democratic system which is failing to engage people. "My start point is the crisis in democracy in Great Britain. I would suggest that the problem is not the people – who are as keen to be involved as ever – but the systems for governance and our democratic structures that are manifestly no longer fit for purpose," he maintains.

So instead the Frome Independents hold their council as public meetings, sometimes with seventy or eighty people turning up and wanting to have a say. It can be, Peter says, 'lively and entertaining and fairly chaotic'. When the time for voting comes it is still only the seventeen councillors who can make the decisions, but the process of getting there seems to be having an effect. The Town Council has not been afraid to use its borrowing powers to acquire key public buildings, including most notably the nineteenth century market hall which has now been rebranded as Cheese and Grain, operating as an arts and music venue, a centre for adult education and a start-up location for small businesses. Peter says that the centre (run as a charitable social enterprise) is profitable, and that it costs the Town Council less to pay the interest on the loan than it previously cost to subsidise the building.

Town and parish councils are the lowest tier of government in England and in many places it can be an unsuccessful struggle to attract enough candidates for elections to be contested. In Frome, Peter maintains, greater activity has had the opposite effect of attracting more interest and engagement. The council is using its powers to build confidence and to attract investment in the town, he says. And, maybe, things will be different again in the future. The aim is not necessarily to hold political power for ever and ever. "Community movements like ours can emerge, be effective, do whatever is necessary and then step down gracefully," the Frome Independents wrote in one of their original public statements. "Perhaps if we get some things right other Independents will emerge during our time in office and they will step into our shoes. Who knows?"

Lunch was over. My route was northwards, making my way up the attractive valley of the Frome river which once upon a time drove the town's woollen textile mills and trying to avoid as much as possible the traffic on the A36. My destination for the evening was a campsite on the eastern outskirts of Bath, high up above the river Avon.

Bathampton

English landscapes are intimately connected with the use of the land for farming, and farming is intimately connected with the food we eat. It seems to me that everyone who enjoys heading off into the countryside for recreation (and for that matter everyone who goes into their local supermarket for the week's shopping) should attempt to understand this. But the farming and food system as it has developed in recent years doesn't necessarily make this a very easy thing to do.

The vast majority of us do not earn our living from the land. Recent figures suggest that around 300,000 people are employed in agriculture, or roughly around 1% of the working population. We've come a long way since George Mitchell's Montacute and the way that agriculture was organised in Britain in the nineteenth century. Farming is continuing to change. The numbers of farms in Britain is going down as the average size of a farm gets bigger. Statistics measure farm size in hectares (a hectare is roughly two and a half acres), and in the UK the average holding recently increased from 56 hectares to 90 hectares in just five years. If you compare British agriculture with that in, say, France, Germany, Spain or Italy you'll find that our farms are significantly bigger than they are across the Channel. In fact, of all the EU countries only the Czech Republic has larger average farm sizes.

There's something else significant about farming in Britain, and that is that the age of farmers is heavily skewed towards those 55 and over. Our farmers are getting older. Some people are concerned at the implications: more should be done to recruit and train a new generation of farmers, they say.

Some people are concerned, too, about food security – or in other words, making sure that, as a country, we have enough safe food available to feed our population. Our island is not currently self-sufficient in food: we produce about 60% of the food we eat (a further 30% of our food comes from the EU). And we don't carry much food in reserve: the country has been estimated to have about three to five days' supply.

Agriculture is, however, heavily subsidised with public money. For all the time that Britain has been in the EU, our farms have been able to claim subsidies under the Common Agricultural Policy, and in recent years this has totalled just short of £3bn each year. The CAP has been controversial: originally it was paid according to what you produced, which led to the famous surpluses of milk and butter and wine and grain. More recently it has been paid according to the size of the land held, which as some cynics have pointed out enables farmers to be paid just for being there and occupying the land. But the subsidy system has also been heavily criticised in some quarters for giving the lion's share of the money to very big landowners. The top 40,000 landowners in the UK own around eleven million hectares, or close to half the country. They have up to now done very well out of the way farming subsidies are distributed.

Of course, with Britain's departure from the EU, the old rules for farming subsidies could be changed and the focus could shift to supporting different priorities. Grants could, for example, be capped, so that the very largest landowners didn't mop up most of the money. At the other end of the scale subsidies could be reintroduced for smallholdings of less than five hectares, which were taken out of the system a few years back. There is an opportunity, in other words, for a real debate about how we want to use quite substantial amounts of public money to support farms, to protect our environment, to preserve our landscapes, and to give us good quality food that doesn't make us obese. Most people, however, expect the former EU arrangements to more or less remain in place. There are, after all, some very powerful lobbies in the countryside who know how to gain the ear of government.

The precise way that government subsidies are paid to farms may not be of immediate relevance to the members of Bathampton Community Co-operative who collectively rent six acres (two and a half hectares) of land a few miles south-east of Bath city centre. What is relevant to the co-op's members is the fact that, by working the land themselves, they are able to know exactly how the food which they eat, or at least some of it, has been grown. I met Alex Robertson and Verona Bass from the co-op on the edge of their land, at the far end of a lane from Bathampton village. As they pointed out, there were fine views to enjoy across the Avon valley just ahead of us to the hills beyond. But in fact there was a pretty good view much closer to hand: just in front of me were beds of healthy-looking vegetables and, beyond them, a series of plastic polytunnels also filled with vegetables. A little further away were some recently planted fruit trees.

What is happening on this plot of land at Bathampton is part of a wider movement of engagement by non-farmers (or, at least by people who are not traditional farmers) in producing their own food. Some towns, following the example of Todmorden in West Yorkshire, have joined the 'incredible edible' network of places where small-scale community growing of vegetables and fruit is actively promoted. Others are linked together in another initiative which goes by the name of 'community supported agriculture'. In each case, the aim is the same: to encourage small-scale, bottom-up ventures which, at least in part, break our reliance on the dominant highly-centralised food and farming industry.

Alex explained to me the history of the Bathampton venture. Their co-operative (or the Dry Arch Growers as they tend to be known in the village, the name coming from an old dry-stone tramway bridge which used to be a local landmark) emerged a few years back out of a wider movement in Bath, Transition Bath, which is working for a sustainable future by supporting moves to a low carbon, locally based economy. Food has been a central focus of Transition Bath. After all, the idea of flying fresh fruit and vegetables around the globe so that our shops can stock, say, asparagus in December or green beans in March isn't precisely a low energy way to do things. Better by far, the argument goes, to see what we can grow ourselves.

The group that coalesced in the autumn of 2010 to form the Bathampton co-operative had something of a lucky break. They discovered that there was land on their doorstep which had for very many years been used for a family-run market garden. The family had let the business drop in the early 1990s, partly because the land was at that time at risk of being compulsorily purchased for a new Bath orbital road, and for the best part of two decades the weeds and brambles had invaded what was once good cultivation land. The idea now was to clear away the brambles, remove the weeds and turn the land back into production. The produce would be sold in veg boxes to members, and although initially all the work would be done voluntarily the target was to produce enough vegetables to be able to employ, at least part-time, a grower. The group reckoned that they needed to be producing around 75 veg boxes a week to get to this break-through position.

A tremendous quantity of brambles and weeds has been removed from the land in the years since they established the co-op and signed the lease, and it has all been done through the co-op members' own hard work.

Having your own land and growing your own produce can be a romantic idea but the reality is that getting land into shape for cultivation can be slow and tedious, a hard graft. So I admired what the co-op had achieved, as I was taken on a guided tour. Several plastic polytunnels had been erected on the foundations of old greenhouses, work that had involved picking tiny shards of glass out of the soil. Arrangements to manage water on the site by catching rainwater and then piping it down to the main vegetable growing areas had been put in place (the alternative, relying on mains water, is both expensive and not precisely environmentally self-sufficient). The co-op had linked up with a Bath-based orchard group who had taken on responsibility for harvesting the existing fruit trees and planting new ones. There was a pen which had been used for keeping pigs and a next-door run for turkeys.

On the other hand, the group are a long way short of that planned-for moment when they will be able to employ someone. The land is now producing enough for around 25 veg boxes a week, and in winter the co-op's own produce has to be supplemented by organic vegetables grown by a commercial grower nearby. Although they have access to a rotorvator, it is a heavy piece of kit that few members can manage, so much of the work continues to be done by hand. Volunteering sessions are held on Thursdays and Sundays, and there is a hard core of perhaps a dozen people who turn out regularly. Still, as Alex tells me, there's never enough people for everything that could be achieved.

So the Bathampton co-operative is now reassessing the way forward. The fashion for veg boxes seems to be passing, so perhaps the right approach is to switch to operating not as a veg box business but as a community allotment. The pigs and turkeys may or may not have a future on the site (feeding the pigs twice a day turned out to be a challenging undertaking in terms of the volunteer rota), and the group are also talking of negotiating with their landlord to return some of the land and to rent in future only part of the site.

The new arrangement, if it is agreed, is likely to mean pushing up members' annual subs from £36 to around £100, so it's a time for taking stock. Alex admits that he has wondered whether it is time for him to move on and to focus just on his own personal allotment elsewhere but he talks of the sense of commitment he feels towards their joint venture. Verona also talks of loyalty to the co-op and to the friends she has made. She talks of the pleasures of working the land: "It's partly about company, and health, and fresh air. It's about the satisfaction of physical work," she explains. It is also, she adds, about keeping skills alive, the skill of knowing how to grow food and look after the soil. Who knows, she says, when our society could need the expertise acquired in small-scale ventures like the one in Bathampton?

Somebody who does understand the value of community-led agricultural efforts like Alex and Verona's co-operative is the farming and food writer Colin Tudge who has coined the term 'real farming' for the way he thinks Britain – and the world – should go. Colin's latest book *Six steps back to the land* offers his thoughts on how to achieve agriculture which is 'expressly designed to provide everyone everywhere with food of the highest standard without wrecking the rest of the world'. Colin, I discovered, lives in a village on the northern outskirts of Oxford, only a few miles off the pencil line which marked my route on my maps, so later on I took the opportunity to call in at his house and talk through the issues with him and his wife Ruth West.

Both Colin and Ruth are in the thick of things when it comes to encouraging different ways of farming and producing food. They are instrumental in the Campaign for Real Farming, in organising the annual Oxford Real Farming Conference (cocking something of a snook at the mainstream Oxford Farming Conference which also takes place each year in the city) and in the embryonic College for Real Farming and Food Culture, which was conceived as a global forum for the exchange of ideas on different ways to approach agriculture.

I explained to Colin and Ruth why I had wanted to look them up. If I was to write about southern English landscapes, I said, I also needed to write about English farming. Could they help me?

It turned out that they could. Colin pointed out that British agriculture has been moving for many years towards a high-technology, high-input industrialised approach to farming. There were farms in East Anglia where holdings of 2000 hectares, with 100 acre fields, were common, he said. Admittedly, he went on, we hadn't reached the situation in some other parts of the world: in Ukraine, he said, there were single farms of more than 300,000 hectares in size, bigger than the size of most English counties. But Colin wasn't convinced that big was better. "Although the thousand hectare arable farm is becoming commonplace, smallholdings and small farms can be far more productive in terms of food per unit area," he told me. "A three hectare holding, or even less, can provide fruit and vegetables, plus eggs, chickens, ducks, pork, bacon and goat's or even some cow's milk."

For him, the key approach is to follow what he calls agroecology. Farming should be low input (or in other words, as close to organic as possible, not relying on agrichemicals), it should be small or medium-sized, diverse (as opposed to reliant on monoculture), and skills-intensive. So we forget the latest GPS-controlled tractors, and get back to ploughing the land by hand? No, he immediately corrects me, that's not it: "A return to small mixed-farms with plenty of farmers does not imply a return to the pre-industrial days when men, women and children did the work of tractors. We also need to develop technologies, both 'high' (science-based) and 'low' (craft-based) appropriate to small complex farms."

"I am advocating small mixed farms not primarily because they are picturesque (although they typically are) but because, when not actively done down, they demonstrably work," he adds.

And how would such a transformation of British farming – Colin calls it the 'agrarian renaissance' which he says we desperately need – affect the food in our shops? The way we think about food needs to change too, he says. "We need to rebuild true food culture, so that people are no longer fixated on convenience and price but also care about quality and provenance." Schools need to offer serious education in food growing and cooking. Initiatives which focus on local growing and cuisine need support. There's got to be a change in our collective mindset, he concludes.

If Colin and Ruth are to get their way, it won't be easy. Farming and food are now big business, and not only in Britain: this is an industry which is tightly integrated into the world of multinational trade. Four companies, I read, have at least three-quarters of the world trade in grain. Seven companies have virtually all the fertiliser supply business. Three firms have almost 50% of the proprietary seeds market. Present-day agriculture is high capital and vast in scale.

The problem with the way things currently are organised is that they don't necessarily seem to be delivering what the human race actually needs, which is the food to enable us to live and thrive. Colin Tudge adds that conventional agriculture is also cruel to livestock and destructive of landscapes and of communities. He argues that it may take a century to achieve the changes he is advocating ("although we haven't got a century," he adds). But, he goes on, "it's remarkable how quickly things *can* change".

Back at Bathampton, I had said my goodbyes to Alex Robertson and Verona Bass and wished their co-operative well. We had been strolling round their land, looking at the work they'd done (and the brambles which were still there in various places, waiting for some more volunteers). We arrived back at a storeroom where bottles of previous seasons' pressed apple juice were being stored. On an impulse, Alex gave me a bottle to take away as a souvenir. It was locally grown and locally bottled. It was, as you would expect, delicious.

Cirencester

It's very hard to arrive in Cirencester except along the route of a former Roman road, but somehow I think I managed it. I had followed the Fosse Way out of Bath, or more precisely from Batheaston, climbing the steep side of the Avon valley, passing the Iron Age fort of Bury Camp and then finding myself in the hidden depths of England's countryside eyeing up that stone cottage I described in my introduction. But in the end, my route diverted from that of the Romans. Twenty miles or so south of Cirencester, I turned my bike eastwards. I had time, and I wanted to visit the small market town of Malmesbury. I padlocked the bike to the side of the railings beside Malmesbury Abbey and went inside.

Coffee breaks may have already featured more than they deserve in this account, but I do have to recommend the coffee and cake in the Abbey. They have placed sofas in one of the transepts of the church where tired cyclists can settle down, replenish their energy levels (I suggest the apple cake, if it's still available), and take in the atmosphere. Because, of course, the real delight of having a coffee here is the opportunity it affords to appreciate the beauty of the building.

Malmesbury Abbey is one of those abbey churches which somehow managed to survive the dissolution of the monasteries so that it isn't now just a pile of stones, green lawns and interpretation boards with National Trust or English Heritage signs. Instead the abbey passed from the hands of the Benedictines to become the town's parish church. Or at least some of the abbey church survived. One of the reasons why the church looks, to be honest, just a little odd in terms of its overall design is that what you see today is only about half of what was once there. For a time in the mediaeval period the building sported both a west tower and – the real jewel – a spire, the spire being the tallest construction in England when it was built, beating Salisbury cathedral's spire by twenty feet or so. But the spire collapsed in a storm around 1500, taking out quite a large part of the original church as it fell. The tower at the west end fell too, at another occasion. The church today is what, originally, was just the church's nave.

Malmesbury is a town with a long human history. A church was founded here (on the same site as the Abbey) in the seventh century. Shortly afterwards, or so the Abbey history tells me, it was equipped with the first organ to be built in England, bellows-blown and constructed on the instruction of the local Christian leader Aldhelm, who was awarded the status of Saint almost as soon as he had died. Later in the Anglo-Saxon period the church was to be the last resting place of King Alfred's grandson King Athlestan. His tomb remains, although the present church came later, built around 1180.

Malmesbury has enough to recommend it to visitors, you'd think, without needing to try too hard, but in recent years it has also promoted itself as Britain's only Philosophy Town, complete with annual philosophy festival. This event certainly has a somewhat different Unique Selling Point from other visitor attractions in the vicinity – the Cotswolds Beer Festival, say, or the annual Bluegrass festival at Kemble airfield, perhaps. But Malmesbury's aim is to celebrate another aspect of its past. Thomas Hobbes, considered one of the founders of modern political philosophy, was born in the town in 1588.

Hobbes' book *Leviathan* came out in 1651, at a time when things could hardly have been more dramatic, politically speaking, in Britain. Parliament had abolished the monarchy and declared the English Commonwealth. Two years earlier Charles I had had his head removed on a scaffold in Whitehall. So Hobbes' treatise, which explores how human societies can be structured and how governments can claim legitimacy, hit the zeitgeist, as you might say. Hobbes argues that, without social and political structures, it is every man for himself. In his most remembered turn of phrase he describes the implications of such a 'state of nature': "No arts; no letters; no society; and which is worst of all, continual fear, and danger of violent death: and the life of man, solitary, poor, nasty, brutish and short."

Hobbes suggests that the answer could be variously rule by monarchy, by aristocracy or by democracy, but in each case the deal is essentially the same: I have to be prepared to give up my right to do things to please and benefit myself and in turn you equally have to give up your own rights. Later this sort of political philosophy was to be developed by Rousseau around the idea of the social contract. Later still, community activists in Frome would find themselves trying to work out in practice just what this thing called democracy might mean.

It was getting on for midday as I finished my coffee but inside Malmesbury Abbey, very quietly, a recording of part of the All-Night Vigil from Rachmaninov was playing. It was time to release my bike and pedal onwards, but I did so with the music still in my head: *Bogoroditse Devo, raduisya, Blagodatnaya Mariye.*

And so to Cirencester. Leominster is *lemster*, Towcester is *toster*, Bicester is *bister* and Beaminster, we have established, is a three syllabic *bemminster*. But Cirencester is Cirencester, said in just the way you might think you should, as a straightforward four syllabic name.

Or at least that's how people pronounce it these days. There was by several accounts an older pronunciation *ciscester*, making a more or less perfect (if confusing) rhyme with Chichester. Yes, said the helpful young woman who took my money at the local museum, I've heard that too. But, she added firmly, it's Cirencester today.

My mother, though, always insisted that the town should be pronounced a different way again. It's *sister* she would say when she heard someone, as she thought, pronouncing it wrongly. Once, when I was much younger, I followed her advice and asked the way from a policeman to 'Sister'. He looked at me very strangely.

My mother's mother's family did come from Gloucestershire, albeit from further to the west of the county, so the valiant attempt in our family to hold fast to *sister* may have originally had some basis in local pronunciation. I can claim in evidence only one jokey limerick which I found online, which seems to imply that the limerick writer used the same pronunciation as my mother. As always with things like this that make fun of English spelling, you have to read it aloud (ending the first line with 'sister').

> There was a young lady of Cirencester
> Who stood up to speak, and they hirencester:
> A man threw a carrot --
> She screeched like a parrot --
> But ducked in a flash, and it mirencester.

Anyway, two thousand years ago it wasn't called Cirencester at all, it was called Corinium Dobunnorum, or simply Corinium. This was a powerful and rich Roman settlement, originally set up as a military fort but becoming by the time of the second century the largest town in Britain after London. The population at that time, it's reckoned, was as much as 15,000, not very far off the size of Cirencester's population today.

The key to Corinium's importance came from the fact that it was the crossroads between several strategically key Roman roads. My new friend the Fosse Way arrived in the town from Exeter and Bath to the south, crossing the town on a SW/NE axis, and leaving for Leicester and Lincoln. Crossing the town on a SE/NW axis was Ermin Street, which in one direction headed to Gloucester, Caerleon and the lands of Wales and in the other made for Silchester (north of modern-day Basingstoke) from where you could choose to head into London or towards the Channel coast.

Corinium also marked the destination for a third Roman road, Akeman Street, which provided a route round the north side of the Thames valley to St Albans (Verulamium) and Watling Street. Akeman Street joined up with the Fosse Way at the town's north-east gate.

If your way lay further north, there was effectively a fourth major highway close at hand. It was just a question of progressing up the Fosse Way towards where Bourton on the Water is today and then switching to Icknield Street, which would lead you to the towns we call Alcester, Redditch, Birmingham, Lichfield, Derby and eventually to Templeborough near Rotherham.

So Corinium was important in terms of its transport links, as effectively the capital of the south and west of the country. From this came economic wealth. Its heyday seems to have been in the fourth century, by which time the town was equipped with all that you'd expect from a major centre of Roman civilisation. The town had at its centre the Forum, an open market place surrounded by colonnaded shops. Nearby was the giant Basilica which served as the administrative centre and courts of justice. There was a large amphitheatre just to the west of the town (the site can be visited today, although it is mostly just the earthworks that have survived). And there were many rich private houses, many boasting mosaic pavements. Over eighty mosaic pavements have been discovered so far in and around the town, several superb examples being on display in the Corinium museum in the centre of the town.

I think I may have described this earlier as the town's local museum, but that it doing it a disservice. The museum has an extraordinarily rich collection of material from the Roman period and is the best place to get a real sense of the town's Roman heritage. It is also the place to discover the town's later history, for Cirencester had another period of wealth and importance in mediaeval times when it was home to a powerful Augustinian abbey, established in the twelfth century and a dominant part of the town's life until the dissolution of the monasteries. Unlike Malmesbury, Cirencester's abbey was almost completely demolished on Henry VIII's orders, however. The abbey's site is in the parkland beyond the church of St John the Baptist, itself a very impressive parish church. There was wealth in the Cotswolds in mediaeval times from sheep, wool and weaving. Cirencester merchants were doing all right for themselves.

Salperton

I stayed in Cirencester overnight at the youth hostel which has recently been opened adjacent to an arts and crafts centre, and was on the road early the next morning. I left the town not by the route of one of the major Roman roads but by the very quiet country road which heads almost due north into the Cotswold countryside, and which goes by the name of The Whiteway. This surely must also have been a Roman road – if not even a pre-Roman route. The Whiteway runs straight and lonely for miles, going nowhere in particular and almost devoid of traffic. Cyclists really can't complain. And when the road gets significantly hillier, as it does near the village of Compton Abdale, well, it's just a question of changing down the gears and cycling a little harder.

If there was wealth in the Cotswolds in times past, it must be said that this remains a part of the English countryside which still exudes a sense of comfortable affluence. The towns and villages have long been on tourist itineraries. It's hard not to be delighted by villages like Bourton on the Water or Upper and Lower Slaughter, or by towns such as Chipping Campden, Northleach and Stow-on-the-Wold.

This is a countryside which is well cared-for, almost manicured. Here's a journalistic quote I stumbled upon: "You can't fail to notice how immaculate the area is. Renovated stone buildings and mown grass verges, it is as beautifully kept as it is beautifully quintessential. This is England's green and pleasant land."

An assertion like that requires some analysis. Why might this seem more quintessentially English than countryside elsewhere? What makes the Cotswold landscape the way it is?

Partly, of course, it comes down to the gloriously creamy warmth of the Cotswold stone – *my* stone, the Jurassic oolite limestone I was following, which in this part of England spreads out beyond its normal narrow boundaries to dominate the geological map of Gloucestershire. The vernacular stone architecture offers a delight to the eye. But it's not just the stone, it's also to do with history. You can argue that many of the towns have an organic unity to them which comes from the fact that they were in their day planned towns –mediaeval 'new towns' which were 'plantations' in the countryside in the period after the Norman Conquest.

Towns such as Northleach, Stow-on-the-Wold, Moreton-in-Marsh and Chipping Campden were never traditional working agricultural villages, of the type which would have been surrounded by large open fields. The Cotswold new towns were set up from the start for trading, with the houses designed for shopkeepers and tradesmen who didn't have to work the lord of the manor's land to pay their feudal dues: they paid their rent in money instead.

Of course, these towns have changed a great deal in eight centuries or so but the skeletal framework of the original planned settlements can still be clearly perceived. Take Northleach, for example, half way between Cirencester and Stow and arguably one of the best surviving examples of a mediaeval new town. Northleach received its market charter in 1227, its property developer – if that is a term we can use for the thirteenth century – being Gloucester Abbey which owned the land. The development was linear, with houses on both sides of the lengthy High Street each having similar sized frontages and each also having their own similarly sized plots of land directly behind. These plots amounted to a quarter of an acre apiece and were calculated according to the measure of distance which older readers may still remember from school days, the measure known as the rod, pole or perch. A rod (or pole or perch) measures 16½ feet, and the plots at Northleach were two rods wide and twenty rods deep. This meant that, to accommodate a town of eighty houses (forty on each side of the main road), you needed a street which was a quarter of a mile long.

Northleach and the other planned Cotswold towns were laid out, in other words, to a carefully devised plan of the kind which a property developer today might submit for a large new estate – although today the houses would be crammed in rather more tightly. The plots are described by historians as 'burgage plots', and even now it is noticeable that as a consequence many of the houses in these towns have the same sized frontages. There was something else about these towns which may be relevant: almost from the start they were self-governing, with a Court Leet headed by a High Bailiff. (Northleach still has its Leet and ceremonially elects a High Bailiff once a year, though it has to be said that their powers are somewhat limited these days.)

If the planned Cotswold towns are part of the story of the Cotswold landscape, the countryside is rather different. I realised this as I found myself cycling through the small village of Salperton, just to the north-west of Northleach. Salperton is a reminder that it's difficult to understand the landscape without also understanding the nature of the way that the land is owned and managed.

Actually, when I first arrived in the village, freewheeling down the hill on the quiet approach road, I thought I might be in luck. It was mid-morning and there were more cars than I would have expected outside one of the buildings beside the road: a café! I anticipated good wholesome country fare: a large slice of chocolate cake, perhaps, washed down with a good strong cup of coffee.

But I was out of luck. Salperton wasn't for me, and indeed I was given a glance by one of the people getting out of their cars which veered on the suspicious. The partridge shooting season had opened a couple of weeks earlier: this was a shooting party, here to see how many birds they could bag.

Salperton is superficially attractive partly because it is an estate village. If you own the estate (and it was sold about twenty years ago to a telecoms businessman from Cheshire for eight million pounds), you acquire not only the magnificent Grade II listed mansion but also thirty-three Cotswold-stone cottages and the tenants who live in them. The new squire bought the estate from its previous owner (who had been involved in the construction trade) who in turn had bought it from Sir Edward Hulton, the publishing magnate who owned Picture Post.

The estate's economy is based on farming and shooting, with the young red-legged partridge birds brought to the site in the Spring and reared there ready for the opening of the shooting season at the start of September. You could claim, therefore, that the birds, like the fields, are effectively being farmed. Later I read an account of a day's shooting at Salperton in a field sports magazine (my quote about England's 'green and pleasant land' comes from the same article) and I realised what I had missed at the café-that-wasn't. Shooting parties (the 'Guns') pay a lot of money for a day's shooting and need properly looking after. If I had been among their number I would have been offered elevenses of champagne, chorizo sausages and home-made sausage rolls. And cake. Oh well.

Salperton, at around 1650 acres, is small as estates go. A much more significant Cotswold landowner is the Bathurst estate at Cirencester. This describes itself as "a traditional family estate with The Mansion at its core which is home to the 9th Earl and Countess Bathurst and extends to approximately 17,000 acres including over 300 residential, agricultural, and commercial properties". The Bathurst's country house is actually almost in the centre of Cirencester, although protected from prying eyes by what is claimed to be the tallest yew hedge in the world, with the estate's lands spreading out into the villages around the town.

Indeed the Bathurst estate owns a large slab of land directly south of Cirencester town centre and this, it has decided, could be just the spot for 2,350 new houses. Outline planning permission was being sought when I was there, and was being vigorously contested by an ad-hoc Save Our Cirencester group. "If they care about Cirencester so much, why are they inflicting a bl*dy great development on us? Oh, yes, money…," was one tweet targeted at the estate which I came across.

So how do we take stock of Cotswold landscapes? We have to understand history and we have to understand land management. If some Cotswold villages can seem quintessentially English – to return to the point we pondered at the start of this chapter – it may well be because these villages are estate villages, with all or almost all the properties managed centrally by an estate management team. Do we therefore have to thank the large estates for protecting England's green and pleasant landscapes? Some might say yes, but in Cirencester some people appear to think the opposite.

Naunton

I was making my way by an extremely roundabout route to Churchill, just over on the Oxfordshire side of the Oxfordshire/Gloucestershire border. Churchill was the Cotswold village which had been the childhood home of the geologist William Smith. Given my focus on following the band of oolite limestone, I felt that I couldn't cycle this way and not give my respects to the great pioneer.

There is a small monument to Smith in the centre of the village put up in the late nineteenth century, but the place where any self-respecting geological pilgrim needs to go if they find themselves in Churchill is down at the bottom of the village, where a small chancel sits alone in a graveyard. The chancel, all that remains of a mediaeval church which was taken down when a new church was erected in the 1820s, was itself threatened with demolition in the 1980s. Villagers came together to save it, and had an idea: the chancel could have a new role in local life, they decided, as the Churchill and Sarsden Heritage Centre. William Smith is, as you'd expect, the main focus of its displays, although he does share the space with another local boy made good, Warren Hastings.

It is true that the old chancel is on the small size: fifteen feet by thirty feet, according to the Chairman of the centre's committee, David Chambers, who came down from his house in the village to open up for me specially. Normally the centre ('possibly the smallest museum in Oxfordshire' is the unlikely marketing message on its website) is open just on summer weekend afternoons. The heritage centre has eight people on its committee as well as a wider pool of local volunteers who are prepared to help out when needed, and David Chambers told me with pride of their recent successful bid for Heritage Lottery Fund support. The grant has meant that they have been able to reequip the centre with exhibition screens and audiovisual films. The AV helps create a proper experience, I think: it means that visits to this tiny museum aren't quite as short as they otherwise would necessarily be.

But before I reacquainted myself with William Smith in Churchill I had had another appointment to keep, and that was to meet Jurassic oolite limestone at very close quarters, courtesy of Julian Palmer. I'd wanted to see for myself how Cotswold stone is quarried and Julian, who runs Cotswold Stone Quarries from his Tinker's Barn quarry just beyond the village of Naunton, was happy to oblige.

It's hard not to warm to Julian. He has spent something just short of fifty years in the quarrying business, starting shortly after he left school at fifteen and going on to build up a very significant business based on stone. Along the way he has had, by his own account, a very colourful life; various marriages have come and gone, and he has also been tricked out of more than half a million pounds by the person who worked for him as his secretary and assistant ("Grandmother flattered by Egyptian toyboy lover steals £500K to spend on man who later disappears" was how the Daily Telegraph covered the story when the case came to court in 2015). Despite this misfortune, Julian shows no sign of being anything other than delighted with the life he has chosen. There are two great things about working in quarrying, he tells me. The first is the finding of the stone. Then, most exciting of all, comes the time when you dig it out. Some people might say that running a quarry is a vocation.

Half way through our conversation he takes me out to his old Landrover, and we drive the few hundred metres from the quarry office up to the rockface. I am suddenly face to face with Great Oolite, and it's an impressive sight.

The stone his quarry is currently extracting is used in various ways, as a building stone, for walling, for crazy paving and particularly for natural roofing slates. Julian Palmer has in his quarry, just below the grassy surface, some of the most densely packed strata of naturally thin oolite stone which can be used more or less as it emerges from the earth as a roofing material. This is what is known as Stonesfield slate, prized for centuries. In the nineteenth century, according to Julian, as many as 36,000 slates could be removed in a week from Cotswold quarries.

These days the rate of removal is not so prodigious but the demand is still there. A few years back, Julian's firm supplied roofing slate for perhaps the most curious Cotswold stone building of them all, the former smithy in Snowshill which was bought by Henry Ford in 1929 and shipped stone by stone to the United States where it now stands in Dearborn near Detroit. Oh yes, Julian tells me, our stone has gone to America, to Japan, to Belgium.

To the M5, too, he adds, since stone from Tinker's Barn has been used in the past few years for the striking new motorway service station near Gloucester.

Working on the quarry face is tough work, I am told. Julian Palmer has done this work in the past but now, not far short of seventy, he employs others to get their hands dirty. I ask him who does the work, imagining that he will tell me of local quarrying families where son has succeeded father for generations in the quarries. No, he tells me, the local boys have all gone. I employ Lithuanians who live in Evesham, he says. I had one or two of them working for me, and I asked them if they had any friends they could bring in. They did.

There are still English people bringing out the Cotswold stone, but at Tinker's Barn the stone that helps create – according to one journalist at least – England's quintessential landscape is likely to be have been hewn from the earth by eastern Europeans.

Adlestrop

A few miles east of Stow-on-the-Wold I stopped the bike at a railway bridge and got off to peer down at the Oxford-Worcester railway line below. I was paying my respects to what just might be the most famous vanished railway station in Britain.

There is no sign of any remains of the platforms which were once there at Adlestrop station. The railway itself is still used – it is marketed as the Cotswold Line, with daytime trains more or less every hour in each direction – but Adlestrop itself was a victim of the 1960s rural railway axe, the station being closed more than half a century ago in 1966.

The reason why it is still remembered today is because of a poem written in early 1915 by Edward Thomas. The poem, simply called *Adlestrop,* is purportedly about a single inconsequential event at a small rural station and yet for many readers it seems to offer something more – an elegiac celebration, perhaps, of the very essence of the English countryside. The poem achieves this in just sixteen lines. Here they are:

Yes. I remember Adlestrop –
The name, because one afternoon
Of heat the express-train drew up there
Unwontedly. It was late June.

The steam hissed. Someone cleared his throat.
No one left and no one came
On the bare platform. What I saw
Was Adlestrop – only the name

And willows, willow-herb, and grass,
And meadowsweet, and haycocks dry,
No whit less still and lonely fair
Than the high cloudlets in the sky.

And for that minute a blackbird sang
Close by, and round him, mistier,
Farther and farther, all the birds
Of Oxfordshire and Gloucestershire.

Thomas was born in 1878 and was in his thirties when he wrote *Adlestrop*. He was to die two years later, having just turned 39, on the western front during the First World War. He was a writer by trade, knowledgeable and keenly interested all his adult life in contemporary poetry, but until around 1913 writing exclusively in prose. He earned his living from journalism and from persuading publishers to commission him to write travel books about journeys taken around southern England. Almost without fail the manuscripts he turned in were not at all the sort of travel books the publishers thought they would be getting. I confess I rather like this part of his character.

Thomas's prose works are probably best described as nature writing. He was strongly influenced by a writer of the previous generation, Richard Jefferies, who had achieved considerable literary success as a nature writer and observer of country life. Thomas, although his family had Welsh roots, was born and brought up in London but when he was in his twenties he moved with his wife Helen and family to live in a series of cottages and houses in the English countryside. He steeped himself in natural history. He was particularly knowledgeable about birds. Here's a taster from his 1906 book *The Heart of England*, to give a sense of his style. It is immediately clear that we are reading the same writer who would later give us *Adlestrop*:

"High up in the beeches, the invisible wood wrens sang, and their songs were as if, overhead in the stainless sky, little waves of pearls dropped and scattered and shivered on a shore of pearls. Below them the wood-pigeons began to coo – with notes that were but as rounded bubbles emerging from the silence and lost again. Just within hearing, in the hawthorn hedge of the wood, blackbirds were singing: they opened with the most high, arrogating notes that slowly rolled on to noble ends, when suddenly they laughed and ceased…"

I should probably also report that for his later book *In Pursuit of Spring* Edward Thomas based his account on a journey through southern England made by bicycle (there are, you will appreciate, really no new ideas to be had in travel writing). "I confess I do like cycling because I get moving air, views and exercise without being reminded of the poorness of my body," he wrote to his wife around this time. Of course, cyclists in Edwardian times had a somewhat different experience on the roads from those of us cycling today: there is one moment in *In Pursuit of Spring* when Thomas, who is somewhere in Wiltshire at the time, feels obliged to report on the fact that "a motorcar overtook me in the village".

Thomas's chosen route, too, was different from mine: he left south London and made his way through Surrey, Hampshire and Wiltshire before ending up on the Somerset coast. He also seems to have had more wet weather than I experienced and he offers an extended writerly riff at one point on the inadequate nature of waterproofs. But the journeying was clearly a delight: "Motion was extraordinarily easy that afternoon," he writes at one point. "No people or thoughts embarrassed me. I fed through the senses directly, but very temperately, through the eyes chiefly, and was happier than is explicable or seems reasonable."

If we are to be at all critical of Thomas's nature and travel writing from this pre-First World War period, it is perhaps that the beauty of the landscapes he describes is refracted through a lens which removes almost all the human economic activity from the countryside. His prose writing is powerful and evocative but the humans who appear in the text – a ploughman here, an agricultural labourer there – do so almost as figures in a landscape painting. There is little sense in his travel writing that the English countryside was at that time experiencing a period of considerable change, or that agriculture had just gone through the deep depression of the later years of the nineteenth century.

This is perhaps surprising, for elsewhere Thomas spells out his view that an understanding of nature and the countryside requires a broader sense of the implications of human activity. Here he is, for example, calling for children to have a proper opportunity to undertake nature study: "...natural history may easily be linked to a preliminary study of hill and valley and stream, the positions of houses, mills and villages, *and the reasons for them*, and the food supply, and so on, and this in turn leads on to – nay, involves – all that is most real in geography and history. The landscape retains the most permanent marks of the past, and a wise examination of it should evoke the beginnings of the majestic sentiment of our oneness with the future and the past, just as natural history should give the child a sense of oneness with all forms of life." Yes, that surely is the challenge facing all of us who attempt to write about the landscape; I have italicised the five words which seem to me the crux of what Thomas is saying, and which would be what I would want to argue too. Don't look just at superficial appearances, look below them for the reasons.

Edward Thomas's turn to poetry came through his friendship with the New England poet Robert Frost who was living in England at the time. (One of Frost's most famous poems *The road not taken* was written about Thomas's own indecision about his life at this time.) Thomas praised Frost's poems for their simplicity of style and lack of traditional poetic rhetoric: "their language is free from the poetical words and forms that are the chief material of secondary poets," he wrote in a review. And Thomas himself then brought exactly the same approach to bear as he began to write his own poetry. One guide to twentieth century English literature draws attention to what Thomas at his best can achieve: "What is in fact subtly organized poetry sounds often like the poet speaking easily but with beautiful precision, revealing an inner life by a remarkably sensitive account of the outer world".

Adlestrop certainly demonstrates this. The poem is based on an actual experience which had taken place some months earlier during a train journey Thomas made from Paddington to Malvern, and which he recorded at the time in a notebook: "Then we stopped at Adlestrop, thro the willows cd be heard a chain of blackbirds songs at 12.45 & one thrush & no man seen, only a hiss of engine letting off steam...". The journey was taken in June 1914, less than two months before war was declared.

When we look at the poem today our reading of it may be influenced by what we know of later history: the appalling loss of life in the First World War (including Thomas himself) after the poem was written or, indeed, our knowledge that Adlestrop station would itself one day be no more. But the poem as Thomas wrote it still has that indescribable note of longing, that sense of elegy.

Adlestrop station has not entirely vanished, however. The former station master's house remains, a substantial brick affair just beside where the down platform would have been. I couldn't help but notice the For Sale sign at the driveway, and later I checked the estate agent's website and downloaded the details. What you could acquire, for a little under £600,000, was a 'bright and beautiful, fabulously individual family home'. The house had been recently given a modern extension: "double doors open out to enjoy far-reaching views across the neighbouring countryside, an eminently sociable space but equally a complete retreat from the busyness of modern life beyond," read the estate agent's copy. Edward Thomas and the poem (with its 'delightful description') were mentioned in the copy, of course, but with a proviso: "A century on, stationmaster and poet might be hard put to recognise the house today".

Yes indeed. But the birds of Oxfordshire and Gloucestershire are still there.

Charterville Allotments

Brize Norton Road in Minster Lovell in northern Oxfordshire is a rather nondescript road with a remarkable history.

I had arranged to stay that night in the outskirts of Witney (in a hotel this time – things were looking up), but I diverted on my way down from Adlestrop and Churchill to have time in Minster Lovell. At this stage of my journey from Dorset to Lincolnshire I was cycling almost due south. Still, my lengthy peregrination round the Cotswolds was approaching an end.

It was in the summer of 1848 that the seventy-eight identical cottages which had been newly built on farmland south of Minster Lovell began to receive their first occupants. They arrived in Charterville, as the new settlement came to be called, from all over the country but particularly from the industrial towns of the midlands and north of England. Charterville represented a new start for them, the chance to put factory life behind and gain independence and self-respect by working the land.

Some of the cottages had two acres of land to cultivate, some three acres and some four, and in each case the newcomers were given a head start in their new life by being provided with a pile of fertiliser manure on their doorsteps. Also erected, just off the main Brize Norton road, was a school-house and meeting room for the fledgling community to use.

Charterville was one of five similar planned communities developed during the later years of the 1840s as part of what is usually described as the Chartist Land Plan. There was Heronsgate (or O'Connorville) near Rickmansworth in Hertfordshire, Lowbands and Snig's End both on the Gloucestershire/Worcestershire border, and Great Dodford close to Bromsgrove in Worcestershire. Charterville was the third to be developed, three hundred acres or so of land having been bought at auction (for £10,378) in June 1847. By September that year the layout of the estate had been planned and the cottages very quickly began to be constructed. They were single-storey but, at a time when working-class people could find themselves living in appalling conditions, were designed to be as good quality as possible. Some people indeed complained that they were *too* good for their occupants. The cottages were symmetrical and had a simple but pleasing elegance, partly created by the central section being extended forward a little and by the small ornamentally designed ventilation stone just below the gable above the front door. There was a central living room with kitchen range and dresser immediately inside the front door and two bedrooms opening up on either side. Behind were a scullery and two other service rooms, one with a copper for washing and one for storage. There were pig sties too, at the rear of the cottages.

At first sight, if you walk down Brize Norton Road today, there can seem to be nothing left of any of this history. But look more closely. It is true that there has been infilling of newer houses over the years but many of the houses still have significant plots of land surrounding them, far more land than you might normally expect. And look at the houses themselves: the basic shape of the original single-storey cottage can in many cases be detected, even if over the years the builders have been in and have built a new front porch, or a first floor extension, or an extra side room. There are also a few – just a few – cottages on Brize Norton Road which look almost the same today as they would have done in 1848. I jotted down their house numbers: 44 and 86 on one side of the road, 45 and 53 and 87 and 93 on the other. But you would find them too, without difficulty.

I turned into Upper Crescent, which had been part of the original estate. Here were other houses clearly showing off their Charterville heritage. And what I also saw here – admittedly very run-down and poorly maintained, but still unmistakeable – was the original two-storey school-house which had been built for the colonists.

The first settlers at Charterville were those who had invested their money into the Chartist Land Plan company and whose names had been drawn at random in a lottery of shareholders. The allocation of land (whether you were entitled to be given a two, three or four acre plot) depended on how much you had invested. We know the names of most of the people who were chosen in this way for a new life in Minster Lovell, for the result of the ballot which took place in February 1848 was published shortly afterwards. Successful names included (to give a few examples at random) W. Hay from Stockport, W. Smith from Newcastle-upon-Tyne, D. Denton from Huddersfield and J. Benson from Manchester. James Beattie came from Glasgow, A. Brierley from Leeds. There were also a few people from closer to hand, including J. Bennett from the Gloucestershire town of Wotton under Edge and E. Tibbles from Cirencester. There must have been a range of regional accents suddenly being heard in what had previously been a small traditional Oxfordshire town.

The Land Plan was one of the manifestations of the powerful working-class movement known as Chartism which mobilised very large numbers of people in Britain in the period between, broadly, 1838 and 1848. Chartism took its name from the People's Charter manifesto which was first agreed in 1838 and which rapidly became the focal point for political activity across the country. The Charter demanded root-and-branch reform of the political system. Its headline demand was for the right to vote to be given to all, regardless of their social class or wealth. (To be precise, the call was normally seen as meaning universal male suffrage, although some parts of the movement campaigned too for women's suffrage.) The Charter also demanded other democratic reforms designed to eradicate corruption and dominance by a political elite. It called for equal sized constituencies, for secret ballots at elections and for representatives who were elected to Parliament as MPs to be paid. The Charter also called for annual Parliaments. The aim was to ensure that Westminster was properly accountable to the electors and that ordinary people without private wealth could afford to stand for election. Almost all the demands of the Charter were, of course, eventually to be won, although not until after much struggle and much passing of time.

Political reform, along the lines demanded by the Charter, was the focus of the first mass petition in 1839 which was signed by 1.3 million people – and summarily rejected by Parliament. A second petition in 1842 was signed by an estimated three million people, but met the same fate. There was a final upsurge of action in 1848, the year when much of mainland Europe was being convulsed by revolutions, when another petition was organised and a mass rally of Chartists took place in south London. The 1848 petition too met with rejection.

But the movement associated with the Chartist period of history was always more than just an attempt to institute change at Westminster. It also encompassed a wider movement by working-class people, particularly in industrial areas, to improve their lot in the here-and-now. It is no coincidence, for example, that the opening of the co-operative grocery shop by the Rochdale Pioneers, recognised as an iconic moment in the development of the British and international co-operative movement, took place in 1844: many of the Rochdale Pioneers were also active Chartists.

And so it was too that the Chartist Land Plan became taken up by many, as a practical way of achieving a better quality of life. Its advocate and the key person behind the development of the five settlements was one of the national Chartist leaders, Feargus O'Connor. It was O'Connor who in April 1845 (at a time when the movement had been suffering considerable persecution and was at something of a low ebb) persuaded the national Chartist conference to agree to the founding of a Chartist Co-operative Land Society. This society, later to go through various name changes, was very much O'Connor's baby. It was he who negotiated the purchase of the five estates and who oversaw the actual layout and construction of the sites. The cottages themselves were, by all accounts, built to O'Connor's own design. He was also the author of *A Practical Work on the Management of Small Farms,* which became the handbook on how the Land Plan colonists could turn their few acres of land to productive use.

O'Connor was charismatic but could also be egotistical, and his role in Chartism has over the years been viewed as controversial. Certainly at the time he proposed the Land Plan the idea was not universally supported among the Chartist leadership. Some people saw it as a distraction from the main struggle, which they argued was to achieve political reform. Why were some of the most forward-thinking working-class activists in industrial areas being encouraged to head back to the land? Nevertheless, at grassroots level, the Chartist Land Plan almost immediately took off. There were, at the peak of its success, at least 70,000 people making weekly subscriptions in part-payment of the shareholding which, when they had finally saved enough, would enable them to participate in the ballot. 20,000 people became shareholders. There were some 600 local branches of the Land Plan across the country and especially in Lancashire and the West Riding of Yorkshire. The money was flooding in.

How were the pioneers at Charterville getting on in the first few months after they moved in? Working the land would have been hard work for people with little or no agricultural experience, and O'Connor had purchased an estate which was by no means ideal for growing: some of the plots had poor-quality soil and the whole area was exposed to wind. There were early tussles between Chartist incomers and the Minster Lovell establishment, as for example in March 1849 when three Charterville residents were barred from standing for the local parish vestry committee. Later local "opulent farmers" – this according to the Chartist newspaper the *Northern Star* – tried to sack the local curate who had opened a school in the school house and who had won the settlers' support. But there were also times of celebration. The *Northern Star* reports an event in May 1848 when, assisted by a local brass band, the community gathered together for a rally following which "after taking of refreshment, a goodly number of both sexes repaired to the school-room, where a ball and concert was held".

Unfortunately for Charterville and its residents, the Land Plan was unravelling nationally. The sad tale of what went wrong has been picked over by historians and can be read elsewhere. There were legal problems in trying to get the land society formally incorporated in law, there was administrative confusion and the ballot arrangement for allocating cottages was also declared illegal. The Land Plan society was subject to a Parliamentary enquiry, and Parliament ultimately in 1851 intervened to wind the venture up. In Charterville itself there was confusion over the legal tenure the settlers had been given. The discovery that part of the original purchase money had been funded by a mortgage loan led to attempts by the previous owners of the land to seek repossession. There were a series of legal actions and evictions. By 1851 only five of the original settler families appear to have been living still in Charterville and by 1867 this figure had fallen to two. Charterville did have an after-life, however: others bought the cottages and allotments, often amalgamating the original plots into larger units of land, some as large as ten or twelve acres. Later in the nineteenth century (and until the general period of agricultural depression) the settlement knew relatively good times, with its prosperity based particularly on the growing of potatoes.

The sad ending of O'Connor's grand dream encouraged social historians for many years to disregard the Land Plan and to focus on the other aspects of the Chartist movement. The venture into land ownership could be written off: as one twentieth century writer put it, it was "absurd and doomed to failure from the start, it took up energy that might have been better spent". But more recently there has been something of a reappraisal by historians. The Chartist Land Plan has been located within the much wider history of radical agrarianism in Britain, spanning several centuries. The impulse behind its popularity at the time when tens of thousands were paying their subscriptions has been reassessed too: one historian who has written on Charterville, Kate Tiller, puts it like this: "It was to restore to working people their God-given right of access to the basic means of survival, the soil. It aimed to get them land, and with it freedom, independence and enfranchisement. It was an alternative to commercialism, to industrial capitalism, to machinery, to the evils of surplus labour."

Indeed, you can place Charterville and the other four Chartist settlements on a long timeline running like a thread through British social history and having its own distinctive effect on the countryside. At the present day the timeline would take us to the community-supported agriculture movement: we'd find it included people like Alex Robertson and Verona Bass of the Bathampton Community Co-operative and their six acres of market garden overlooking the river Avon. Travelling backwards in time, we would pass through the back-to-the-land and self-sufficiency movements of the 1970s and 1980s (the time when Tom and Barbara were seeking The Good Life every week on television). We would note the efforts taken between the two world wars to produce council housing on suburban estates where all had access to generous sized gardens and, before that, we would watch from the Strangers' Gallery in the House of Commons in 1908 as the Small Holdings and Allotments Act was passed. This instituted a requirement on county councils to acquire land where appropriate to enable families to settle on the land and was a direct governmental response to the 'land question' agitation which had been a feature of the end of the nineteenth century.

Further back again, we would come across the campaigners for land reform and land nationalisation, the Land and Labour League and the Land Tenure Reform Association. This was the time when some at least thought the answer to industrial unhappiness and unrest was to relocate workers in the countryside and equip them – as the slogan of the time had it – with 'Three acres and a cow'. Earlier still, before we arrived back at Charterville and Feargus O'Connor's Chartist Land Plan, we would encounter the Freehold Land Societies of the mid-Victorian years.

But we would find that the timeline took us back before the Chartists as well. We would note the efforts in the decades immediately before Chartism of early socialists to establish their own co-operative settlements on the land (perhaps today these would have been given the name of communes). We would be taken to see how they got on, in places such as Ralahine in Co Clare, Orbiston near Motherwell, and Manea Fen in Cambridgeshire. We'd hear the view expressed that the land of Britain should, by rights, be held by all – that it should be 'the people's farm'.

The timeline can be traced back even further, back to the middle of the seventeenth century, as I was to discover for myself when my bicycle and I arrived in Wellingborough. But Wellingborough was still several days' journey away. For the time being, I was ready to take the busy main road back from Charterville and Minster Lovell into Witney, to find my hotel for the night.

Some weeks later, however, when my cycle was safely stored at home, I was back on the trail of the Chartists and their land settlements. This time I was not in Oxfordshire but in Worcestershire. I took the car down to Great Dodford, the last of O'Connor's five sites, to see for myself what the inside of one of the Chartist cottages would have looked like in the late 1840s. In Charterville the Chartist properties are privately owned and all I could do was gaze from the road. By contrast one cottage at Great Dodford is open for visitors, owned by the National Trust. The cottages here (like those at Heronsgate, Lowbands and Snig's End) were almost identical to those constructed in Charterville: O'Connor had clearly hit on a design which he liked.

It's perhaps symbolic of the renewal of interest in the Chartist Land Plan that in 1997 the NT decided it was appropriate to acquire Rosedene cottage in Great Dodford and to restore it to how it would have been when it was first built. It's a fascinating experience to be taken inside and to see how the cottage would have looked when their original occupiers first arrived, and the local volunteer guides who were on duty the day I was there did an excellent job in introducing Feargus O'Connor and explaining the background to Chartism.

Of course, it would be fair to say that Rosedene is hardly top of the NT's league table when it comes to places the public want to see. These days Rosedene is opened for just one Sunday afternoon a month, so by my calculation perhaps a hundred people a year take advantage of the opportunity to visit. By contrast, the NT's Montacute House attracts about 100,000 people each year (and another 50,000 stop to explore the grounds and the tea-room). But you can argue that English history is as much about Rosedene and the Chartist settlements as it is about Montacute House and all the other country houses. It's important, I'd say, that the Chartist Land Plan settlements are not completely forgotten.

Blenheim Palace

It's funny how land in the English countryside can be turned to all kinds of different uses.

When the first settlers arrived in Charterville in 1848, they probably didn't realise that they had become relatively close neighbours of the Duke of Marlborough, whose Blenheim estate at Woodstock was ten miles or so away on the other side of Witney. They had their two, three or four acres of Oxfordshire land to tend. The Blenheim estate runs to something over 12,000 acres today; in the nineteenth century it was even bigger, at about 22,000 acres.

Blenheim is named after the battle which took place in August 1704 near the small village of Blenheim, Bavaria (except that in German the village's name is Blindheim). This was one of the key battles in what was called the War of the Spanish Succession, a war which (probably with good reason) most of us today would be hard-pressed to describe. It was, you could say, one of the apparently endless series of major conflicts between the European nations which have racked our continent over the centuries, when the great powers turned to military muscle to try to maximise their own political advantage and reduce that of their rivals.

The War of the Spanish Succession was an occasion when Britain was pitched against France. Britain was part of an alliance which included Austria and the Dutch Republic. France had Bavaria as an ally. The prize being fought over was who was to get their preferred candidate on to what was then the disputed throne of Spain. In the end, after several bloody battles, the conflict was resolved through compromise and Anglo-French negotiation.

Whatever it was like for the soldiers who fought the battles or for the locals living in the lands the armies fought over, the War of the Spanish Succession was the making of John Churchill. It was Churchill, the First Duke of Marlborough (he had been elevated to the dukedom a short time earlier, in 1702), who led the British forces to victory both at Blenheim and at some of the later battles.

Marlborough's battlefield success merited the thanks of a grateful nation, it was decided, and the government resolved that the thank-you in this instance would be to give the Duke a properly impressive country mansion and park. Blenheim was the result.

I had arranged to meet John Hoy, the current chief executive of Blenheim Palace, early in the afternoon so I had time in the morning to explore the parkland and to take the guided tour of the house. I started by wandering up to the forty-metre high Column of Victory which you reach at the end of an avenue of elms which starts at the main courtyard of the Palace itself. If you are going to have a Column of Victory on your land, I decided when I got there, it's probably not necessary to go in for any bashfulness or false modesty. I wrote down some of the words on the inscription at the bottom of the column:

"John Duke of Marlborough
The hero not only of his Nation but his Age
Whose Glory was equal in the Council and in the Field
Who by Vision, Justice, Candour and Address
Reconciled various and even opposite interests...
Who by Military Knowledge and irresistible Valour
In a long Series of uninterrupted Triumphs
Broke the Power of France"

That more or less sorts out all that you need to know about the first Duke of Marlborough, if not about the niceties of the politics of the War of the Spanish Succession.

Blenheim Palace has been politely described as 'monumental'. My tour guide in the house later on would talk of the 'imperious self-confidence' it exudes. At the risk of alienating some of my readers, I would describe it as pretty ugly. There are many exquisitely fine country houses dotted across England's countryside, but in my opinion Blenheim doesn't count among them. (In my defence, I have to say that Blenheim has long been a controversial building: many architectural experts over the past three hundred years have tended towards the same view as me. Some people like the building, though.)

Blenheim could have been built by Sir Christopher Wren, in which case the story might have been different. John Churchill's wife Sarah, the formidable Duchess of Marlborough, was rooting for Wren to get the commission but the Duke himself had met the architect and dramatist Sir John Vanbrugh (apparently by chance at a theatre) and it was to Vanbrugh that he gave the work. Vanbrugh had recently completed the grandiose Castle Howard in Yorkshire. Blenheim was built in the short-lived architectural style known as English Baroque.

The actual construction of the Palace was beset with financial problems. It was never precisely clear just how deep the pockets of a grateful nation would turn out to be, and the Parliamentary vote to fund Blenheim unfortunately (for the Duke) did not spell out the financial details. Public funding dried up altogether in 1711, six years after Vanbrugh had been given the commission, when the Duchess of Marlborough fell out with the then Queen, Queen Anne. Later the Duke resolved to finish the incomplete Palace at his own expense. When he died in 1722 the Duchess took charge, instituting economies and bringing in Nicholas Hawksmoor as Vanbrugh's assistant. The building was eventually completed in the 1730s.

Blenheim was built to awe, and a building like this requires enormous sums of money. The Marlboroughs hit severe financial trouble in the middle of the nineteenth century and the estate was only rescued when the 9th Duke arranged a loveless marriage with the American heiress Consuelo Vanderbilt. Vanderbilt brought as her dowry the equivalent at today's prices of $75m. The estate was saved, although the marriage ended in divorce. However, the effects of earlier straitened times remain. The state rooms (the main part of the guided tour of the house now for visitors) lost many of their treasures in the nineteenth century when paintings by artists such as Raphael, Rubens and Van Dyck were sold, as were the 18,000 volumes in the library. The wall hangings now are predominantly tapestries commissioned by the first Duke, showing him in various different military situations but almost always doing down the French. Visitors to the house end their tour in the impressive library, 180 feet (55 metres) long which was originally built as a picture gallery.

I have been impolite about the architectural merits of the Palace. What, however, about the parkland which surrounds the building? Something like 2,000 of Blenheim's total 12,000+ acres have been dedicated to the park and they remain today an impressive testament to the extraordinary skill of the landscape architect Lancelot Brown ('Capability' Brown).

Brown was brought in to remodel the parkland at Blenheim in the 1760s and, as elsewhere, he set about undertaking major groundwork to make the landscape more 'natural'. Trees were moved or planted, hills and valleys rearranged and – Brown's greatest *coup de théâtre* – the tiny river Glyme was dammed and a huge serpentine lake created. It was a stunning achievement.

If you visit Blenheim, you'll find one of the interpretation boards for visitors will tell you the following: "This landscape is still, as Brown intended, one of the most beautiful landscapes in England". This is a pretty bold claim and is it one we should accept? I was reminded of a newspaper article about Capability Brown I had come across at the time of the tercentenary of his birth, in 2016, which put it like this: "Lancelot 'Capability' Brown has so comprehensively infiltrated our national consciousness that our notion of what is beautiful in the English landscape is almost entirely of his making". I think the author is right. The point to bear in mind, of course, is that the beauty of Blenheim's parkland (and it is beautiful) is entirely the result of artifice – highly skilled artifice, but artifice nonetheless.

There is very little that reorders the English landscape more dramatically and more radically than the construction of a country estate. As we have seen, Brown had access to two thousand acres or so to mould to his vision – in effect to rebuild the land as he wished. But it should be added that the land on which the Blenheim estate was constructed was historically given over to what can be seen as the mediaeval equivalent of eighteenth century parkland. Before the government presented it to Marlborough, it had previously been used for centuries as a royal deer park. There is evidence going as far back as Anglo-Saxon times that kings had kept this land as a 'forest' (not necessarily a forest with trees in the modern sense but rather a game reserve with its own strict forest laws). One author suggests King Alfred may have hunted here, and there is certainly confirmation that this was a royal forest at the time of the Domesday Book. Later an old hunting lodge stood on the site. The remains of the lodge were cleared away to make way for the new Blenheim Palace.

So Capability Brown did not have to do here what he and other landscape architects elsewhere in the country at this time were doing, and that was to remove whole villages and their farmland in order to create the neatly manicured parkland which landowners had come to expect. Brown did just this, for example, in mid-Dorset when the Earl of Dorchester asked him to landscape the grounds surrounding his house, Milton Abbey. The existing village Middleton was demolished and a new estate village, Milton Abbas, built at a more discreet distance from the Big House.

I have been putting forward the view at various points in this book that, to appreciate properly the English landscape, you need to understand the economics behind the view. Capability Brown received the commissions he did because those with large landholdings, both members of the long-established aristocracy such as the Duke of Devonshire (Chatsworth House) and the Earl of Coventry (Croome Court) but also those such as the Duke of Marlborough who had more recently acquired their titles and their estates, had the economic power which came from the income the land provided. Marlborough, who as plain John Churchill had come from the ranks of the minor gentry rather than the upper class elite, was able to afford Blenheim in part thanks to state money. A century on, the 5th Duke of Marlborough's lavishly exuberant enthusiasm for spending money left the estate in dire straits.

What are the economics behind Blenheim Palace today? The person who has the ultimate responsibility for bringing in the income to meet the outgoings is John Hoy, who met me in the modest office he was occupying at the Woodstock end of the Blenheim estate. Hoy has been chief executive here since 2003, having come to Blenheim with the sort of track record which eminently qualifies you for a job like this. He is a qualified chartered surveyor who was educated at a public school in Cambridge and then for three years at the Royal Agricultural College. He worked as the Assistant Agent at the Goodwood estate in Sussex and then as the Agent of the Knebworth estate in Hertfordshire. But he has also had direct senior management experience of what we could best describe as visitor attractions: Warwick Castle, where he was Head of Operations and Retail, and then General Manager of Madame Tussaud's in London.

This is relevant because Blenheim is a business of two distinct halves. On the one hand, it is a major estate which needs managing in the usual way by a land agent. Most of the 10,000 acres or so which are not part of the immediate Blenheim parkland is farmed, which means that the estate has a large number of tenant farmers, both those who hold the land on pre-1966 Agricultural Holding Act terms and those who hold Farm Business Tenancies (which are more flexible for landlords and where there are no rights of succession). We have at Blenheim, John Hoy says, a variety of tenants, some good, some less good.

As with many country estates, the land is also used for shooting. Indeed, the shooting agency which will book you a day's partridge shooting at Salperton will also sign you up for a day at Blenheim. "Shooting at Blenheim is something special in itself, with many drives taking place within the parkland. Lunch is taken within the Palace and guns are offered a private tour of the palace at the end of the day," read the marketing copy I came across. The estate also produces an income from forestry, and there are over 2,000 acres of mature woodland on the estate.

But the other part of the Blenheim business is quite different. As well as being a land estate, Blenheim Palace is in the tourism and visitor economy sector. This requires a set of different skills, not to mention a strong streak of entrepreneurialism.

Hoy recounts with some pride the way he has overseen a striking increase in visitor numbers over the time he has been in post, up from around 300,000 a year to 800,000 and more. When he arrived, he says, the estate was only open in summer months and had no marketing or sales team. The attitude, he says, was "We are Blenheim Palace, if we open the gate people will come", an approach which could only go so far. Now Blenheim welcomes visitors throughout the year, every day except Christmas Day.

It's not cheap: a standard adult visitor day ticket cost just short of £25 when I was there, although this can be converted without further payment into an annual pass. (Of course, if you stick to the rights of way you can walk through the estate for nothing.) But Hoy and his colleagues know that they can't rely just on the traditional country house visitor. There are endless events and festivals organised. There's a jousting tournament, a flower festival, a classic cars rally, international horse trials, a triathlon, a half marathon, and much more. It all helps to bring in more visitors. Take the triathlon, for example: the event doesn't just attract hundreds of competitors, their families and friends come along, too.

There are other income streams. Blenheim Palace is available for weddings, banquets and receptions. The estate has a mineral water business, bottling its own water on the estate. Very helpfully, the estate is frequently used as a location for films and the location fees can be substantial. Films in turn boost visitor numbers. ("We have a lot of filming income, and then afterwards we benefit from film tourism," John Hoy explains.) It all helps increase the top half of the income and expenditure account.

Blenheim Palace remains the home (or one of them) of the Duke of Marlborough. We have now reached the 12th Duke, Jamie Spencer-Churchill, who succeeded to the Dukedom in 2014. "My wife, children and I are very pleased to welcome you to our home and hope you will enjoy an inspiring day out with us," the Duke writes in the main tourist leaflet given to visitors (or at least he puts his name to the text: it's always possible that somebody in John Hoy's team wrote the welcoming message for him). The family rooms are in one of the wings, not in the part of the palace the visitors see, but I was told that the Duke and his family tend to be there in the autumn and winter months when the shooting is taking place. Of course though Blenheim remains the Duke of Marlborough's home the legal ownership is now carefully separated off in a trust arrangement.

It is the visitor economy side of the business which is used to fund the necessary maintenance and restoration work on the Palace and park, John Hoy says, and perhaps predictably he would like more than he currently gets. He would like £5m properly to restore Queen Pool (the top end of Capability Brown's artificial lake), he tells me. He would like £3m for other forthcoming restoration work – in fact, he says that £40m is really what's needed for a properly planned ten-year programme of maintenance. At the moment his business is providing income of around £2m a year. But – as well as the constant push to dream up new events and marketing initiatives – Hoy has two ways in which Blenheim Palace can significantly increase the money it has available.

Firstly – in something of a return to the origin of the Blenheim story – there is money coming once again from the taxpayer. In 2016 a new charity, the Blenheim Palace Heritage Foundation Charity, was established. Visitors can now Gift Aid their entrance fee to the charity – and that means that the government will step in and add 25p for every £1 given. John Hoy cautiously suggests that Gift Aid could contribute an extra half a million pounds a year to the pot of money he has available. Of course, it could be argued that at a time of austerity there might be better ways to spend half a million pounds or more of public money than to help subsidise a country estate, but that might seem to be a little churlish. Blenheim Palace is, after all, one of UNESCO's World Heritage Sites I talked about at the start of this book. Let's just say that the British people's thank-you present to the victor of the Battle of Blenheim is still on-going.

Establishing a charity also means that Blenheim is potentially eligible for grants from the Heritage Lottery Fund, a valuable source of future funds which, as a privately owned estate, Blenheim could not previously access.

John Hoy's other lucky break is the urgent need in the country, and particularly in the Oxfordshire area, for more housing. It's well known that, once land is reallocated from agriculture to housing, its value goes through the roof. Government statistics suggest that a hectare of agricultural land in England is worth on average about £21,000, whereas industrial land potentially available for housing can easily be worth half a million a hectare, and typically is over a million pounds in the South East. If you are a major landowner – as the Blenheim Palace estate is, thanks to the original gift of the estate – and if you can negotiate with the planners to convert a small amount of your total holding into housing, you are in line for a significant windfall. John Hoy says that the millions which the estate may realise will be put into an endowment fund. "We have a shortage of housing. We'll put the money to good use," he adds.

Steeple Barton

From Blenheim and Woodstock my way was east but I began with a short detour northwards, along a series of quiet Oxfordshire back roads to the group of villages known collectively as The Bartons. Steeple Barton, I decided, deserved a visit.

I mentioned in the introduction the book by W.G. Hoskins *The Making of the English Landscape.* Hoskins' book, which first came out in 1955, has had a profound effect in the years since then. His painstaking work in getting under the surface of the English countryside to disclose its historical roots – to explain why fields and boundaries and settlements are there today in the way that they are – inspired later generations of researchers and could be said to have launched into prominence the fledgling disciplines of both landscape archaeology and landscape history. Hoskins himself became the editor of a series of works by other writers on the landscape histories of individual English counties, and he had a brief moment of glory later in his life in the 1970s with a BBC TV series on landscape *One Man's England.*

Hoskins wrote *The Making of the English Landscape* in Steeple Barton, his home at the time, and the village (although not named) features in the book's concluding chapter, one of the most personal sections of the book. Hoskins has been setting out, over the previous three hundred pages or so, the thesis that when it comes to understanding the English landscape, in his own words, "everything is older than we think". He draws the threads together at the end by taking Steeple Barton as an example. Here is how he starts this section:

The view from this room where I write these last pages is small, but it will serve as an epitome of the gentle unravished English landscape. Circumscribed as it is, with tall trees closing it in barely half a mile away, it contains in its detail something of every age from the Saxon to the nineteenth century. A house has stood on this site since the year 1216, when the bishop of Lincoln ordained a vicarage here, but it has been rebuilt over and over again, and last of all in 1856. Down the garden, sloping to the river, the aged and useless apple trees are the successors of those that grew here in the time of Charles I, when the glebe terrier of 1634 speaks of 'one orchard, one backside, and two little gardens'. Beyond the apple trees and within a few feet of the river is a large raised platform, visible in winter before its annual submergence in weeds, part of a vanished building, and there are clear lines of stone walls adjoining it. Almost certainly this is the site of one of the three water-mills recorded on the estate in Domesday Book...

And so Hoskins continues, talking of the damp hollow full of sedge across the stream which he identifies as a fishpond recorded in an early charter; the hedges he can see, some dating from the mediaeval enclosed pasture which was in the village from the early 1200s; the parish church, rebuilt in 1300 perhaps on the site of a Saxon church. "And then, finally, out of sight but only fifty or sixty yards from this room, in the field next the garden, there lies buried the main street of the old village that was wiped out by the Black Death."

Hoskins was a Devon man, born in Exeter in 1908 and dying in Cullompton in 1992. He taught economic history at a number of universities, and indeed was Reader in economic history at Oxford University when he was living in Steeple Barton. He is particularly associated with Leicestershire, however, where he taught at the University of Leicester and where he was to finish his academic career as Professor of English Local History. His interest in research into the history of rural areas (including individual parishes) was partly developed in the 1930s and 1940s when he led adult education classes in Leicester in the subject.

The reason why *The Making of the English Landscape* can appeal today, more than sixty years after it was written, is in part because it can be seen as a detective work. Hoskins offers two particular techniques for uncovering the history of the landscape. The first is a forensic scrutiny of maps. "There are certain sheets of the one-inch Ordnance Survey maps which one can sit down and read like a book for an hour on end, with growing pleasure and imaginative excitement," he wrote. "One dissects such a map mentally, piece by piece, and in doing so learns a good deal of local history, whether or not one knows the country itself."

Hoskins was not alone in using maps in this way. Two years before his own book another academic O.G.S. Crawford had brought out *Archaeology in the Field* which proposed an approach to archaeology focused less on traditional excavation and more on research work which could begin with the study of modern and historical maps in local record offices. What can maps tell us? Hoskins advised his readers to explore among other things the "delicate nerve-like complexity of roads and lanes", "the siting of the villages and hamlets" and "the way the parish boundaries fit into one another".

The importance of boundaries was a particular theme of Hoskins – indeed he argues, I think convincingly, that boundaries and boundary hedges and ditches can be some of the most ancient features in the English landscape.

Hoskins' second technique was to get out and simply walk the countryside, to see what he could see. Here is his account of research work he undertook in relation to Anglo-Saxon estate boundaries:

By the time one has scrambled over hedges, leapt across boggy streams in deep woods, traversed narrow green lanes all but blocked with brambles and the luxuriant vegetation of wet summers, not to mention walked along high airy ridges on a day of tumultuous blue-and-white skies with magnificent views of deep country all round – by the time one has done this, armed with a copy of a Saxon charter and the 2½- inch maps, the topography of some few miles of the English landscape is indelibly printed on the mind and heart. And at the same time, one has the... mental excitement of making some unmistakable identification and of revealing to oneself the age of some ordinary feature of the scene – a ditch, a hedge, a piece of marsh, a pond, or what you will.

Not many of the readers of *The Making of the English Landscape* will necessarily have the research skills to read Anglo-Saxon or mediaeval charters, but I think we can all imagine ourselves trying to decipher the code of the countryside by poring over OS maps or getting our boots on and walking the hedgerows. So, while Edward Thomas in *Adlestrop* offers an interpretation of the English landscape through a poet's sensibility, Hoskins seems to offer a more rigorously academic way of understanding landscape. What we have today, he demonstrates, is the accumulated evidence of centuries of human occupation of the land. *Everything is older than we think.*

Nevertheless academics have more recently subjected Hoskins' work to some further scrutiny and we should do likewise. Hoskins brought his own concerns and prejudices to his work, and we need to be conscious of how these may have affected his approach to the landscape.

What an English village pub should look like? The Three Horseshoes at Burton Bradstock

Cider country

St Mary's Church, Loders

Delivering the post in Powerstock

Some local services are disappearing: the telephone box at Powerstock

Beaminster at night

The Helyar Almshouses at East Coker were built between 1640 and 1660

A lane near East Coker

The river at Bradford on Avon, once an important woollen textile centre

Norton Manor near Malmesbury

A detail from the archway of the South Porch entrance to Malmesbury Abbey

Cirencester, the Romans' Corinium Dobunnorum, as it is today

Julian Palmer at his Tinker's Barn quarry in the heart of the Cotswolds

All that remains of the old church at Churchill, now possibly the 'smallest museum in Oxfordshire'

One of the original Chartist cottages at Charterville near Minster Lovell

A natural English landscape? How the parkland at Blenheim Palace looks today, thanks to the efforts of Lancelot ('Capability') Brown

The Cube in Corby

The Cotswolds in north Northamptonshire? One of the main streets in Oundle

A side street in Oundle

No longer the village post office

The poet John Clare's statue in his native village of Helpston

Inside the village shop in Collyweston, run as a community co-operative

Stamford at night

The Humber estuary at Winteringham

One archaeologist and university professor who admits to have been personally inspired by Hoskins' work has put it like this: "While as an economic historian he was quite aware of the harsh realities of rural life, it is clear that Hoskins's view of the English landscape was a nostalgic and even sentimental one that was profoundly anti-modern in its tenor".

Is this fair? Certainly Hoskins was uncomfortable with the modern world he found himself living in. Every single change in the English landscape since 1914, he wrote in *The Making of the English Landscape,* has either 'uglified it or destroyed its meaning'. (It is, he added, a "distasteful subject".)

This is Hoskins, I think, allowing himself momentarily to depart from scientific rigour. His opinion is certainly contentious. I can think of all sorts of developments in the twentieth century (even if we stop at 1955, the year of the book's publication) which can be seen as positively enhancing the landscape that Hoskins loved. The creation of national parks and of AONBs (Areas of Outstanding Natural Beauty) would be one example. The nature conservancy steps taken after the Second World War, including the creation of a network of national nature reserves and SSSIs (Sites of Special Scientific Interest), would be another. The requirement on local authorities in England and Wales to map and manage footpaths and other rights of way would be a third: this change not only allowed greater public access to the countryside but it also directly helped to preserve historic tracks and paths. Then I could mention the tighter planning controls which were gradually introduced as the twentieth century progressed, which led to restrictions on unsightly ribbon developments and incursions into the green belt. If I was to allow myself to include the rest of the twentieth century after 1955 my list would be even more extensive. I'm sorry, but I think Hoskins' diatribe against the twentieth century looks a little thin.

Besides, he should have been cautious in suggesting that his own time was somehow unique, because as a historian he would have been aware that earlier changes which we now accept as part of the history and heritage of the landscape had also in their time been subject to fierce criticism. We'll be tackling the issue of eighteenth and nineteenth century enclosures later in this book so let's mention another example. The construction of railway lines criss-crossing the country, with their extensive earthworks, embankments, cuttings, bridges and tunnels, was undoubtedly seen by some observers at the time as making the landscape 'uglified'. (Interestingly, Hoskins' twentieth century assessment was that the railways "created as much beauty as they inadvertently destroyed".)

Hoskins has left himself open to criticism, therefore, that his version of the English landscape is a value-laden one, one which is attractive for a middle-class audience living in the countryside but which may have less to offer other sections of our society. He has also been criticised for not putting the landscape he describes in its broader (global) economic perspective in order to identify, say, the effects of the mass emigration off the land by those who had once worked it or of the origins of the wealth of many Georgian country parklands in the slave trade.

I think what we have to do is put *The Making of the English Landscape* in the historical context in which it was written, the 1950s. This was a time when Britain was still recovering economically and psychologically from the traumas of the Second World War and was enmeshed in the anxieties of the atomic age and the Cold War. A celebration of the not-quite-but-almost-timeless beauty of the countryside such as Hoskins offered was something that could catch the mood of the times.

What about us here today? For all of us for whom England is our country, I would suggest that we share a need for a sense of collective history and for a sense of a landscape which we recognise as our own and which we can all appreciate. This is a political and cultural challenge, and I'd say that it's one which is becoming increasingly important as the concept of Englishness comes actively up for discussion. Hoskins' approach takes us part of the way there and his achievement in popularising English landscape history should certainly be recognised. But we need other voices as well. The view from the window in Steeple Barton is only one way to see England.

Juniper Hill

If I ever find myself with national responsibility for improving provision for cyclists on Britain's roads, I will start with the south Northamptonshire town of Brackley.

I'm sorry to be negative, Brackley. You are a pleasant market town. You have some attractive buildings, and you show off Jurassic limestone as a building material almost as well as the more obviously touristy Cotswold towns. You have, I noticed, a well-stocked independent bookshop, something which authors always like to see. And I've got fond memories of visiting you when I was younger, for it was here that one of my godparents lived for much of her adult life. But there is one serious problem which you have got to acknowledge: you are fearsomely difficult to get to for any cyclist coming from the south.

Many places have approach roads which are snarled up with heavy flows of traffic, but most places also have B-roads or quiet back ways which will get you safely into their town centres. Careful reading of the road map is all that's needed. It worked for me in Frome, in Cirencester and Witney. But it didn't work in Brackley.

Instead, I found myself deposited off the country road I had been following at a roundabout on the A43 bypass several miles south of Brackley. Once upon a time, I'm sure, my by-road had gone straight into the town. But someone, when they had planned the A43, had thought they would tidy up the road network. What they perhaps hadn't taken into account is that the A43, as a major through-route between the M1 and the M40, is a dual carriageway road effectively acting as a motorway. Lorries and cars fly past. Cyclists get treated as strange interlopers.

I did my best. I made a six or seven mile detour round to the south-west of the town in an attempt to avoid the trunk road. My route took me past the curious excrescences on the landscape which are RAF Croughton, an electronic eavesdropping station which (despite the RAF name) is linked to the US signals intelligence National Security Agency and which, it has been suggested in the national press, played a role in the US's clandestine monitoring of other countries' embassies. But I didn't stop to make any journalistic enquiries: I felt I wouldn't have been warmly welcomed and I was by that stage anxious to get to Brackley.

My detour was in vain. I found myself back on the A43, only a mile or so north of where I had been originally. There was nothing for it. I took my life in my hands. I survived.

Perhaps the traffic on the A43 seemed particularly frantic because all that morning my roads had been completely quiet. I cycled from Steeple Barton westwards, passing over the Oxford Canal at Lower Heyford and avoiding Bicester by going through Middleton Stoney, Bucknell and Bainton. I found myself at one stage on a road so little used that there was grass growing through the tarmac in the centre. And then another surprise: a road sign warned me that there was a ford ahead, which I splashed my way through.

I'd chosen this route in order to visit Lark Rise, the hamlet which was the childhood home of Flora Thompson and which she wrote about much later in life in her trilogy published as *Lark Rise to Candleford.* Or, more accurately (since Lark Rise is the fictional name which Flora Thompson gave to the place where she grew up), I was visiting Juniper Hill.

Flora Thompson was born in Juniper Hill in 1876. Here is how she introduces it at the start of her first book, called simply *Lark Rise:* "The hamlet stood on a gentle rise in the flat, wheat-growing north-east corner of Oxfordshire. We will call it Lark Rise because of the great number of skylarks which made the surrounding fields their springboard and nested on the bare earth between the rows of green corn. All around, from every quarter, the stiff, clayey soil of the arable fields crept up; bare, brown and windswept for eight months out of the twelve… Only for a few weeks in later summer had the landscape real beauty."

I can't say I found Lark Rise/Juniper Hill a place of particular beauty, either, but perhaps that was because I wasn't there at the right time to see the golden wheat ready for harvesting. And I saw no skylarks. Large arable fields today surround a smattering of houses and the one road through the hamlet is straight and dull (if nicely empty of fast traffic). Juniper Hill itself has lost the inn which was there in Flora Thompson's childhood and which (given that the church and school were in the next-door village of Cottisford) was the only community building of any kind, even if it was in her day resolutely a place for the men of the settlement only.

But the attractiveness or otherwise of Juniper Hill is not the point. Juniper Hill has a place in English social history because of the success of Flora Thompson's evocation of a country way of life as it was in the 1880s, a way of life that had gone for good when she published *Lark Rise* in 1939 and her two follow-up books a few years later. "This country scene is only a little over fifty years distant from us in time; but in manners, customs and conditions of life, it is centuries away," she wrote. Today the world of Juniper Hill in the 1880s seems even more remote from us. Nevertheless, the world she depicts has had an after-life, firstly in 1979 and 1980 when *Lark Rise* was dramatised for the National Theatre, and then more recently with the transformation of the three books into the BBC costume drama *Lark Rise to Candleford* which ran over four seasons from 2008. The BBC, quite understandably, allowed itself considerable licence in the adaptation of the books for television but the books themselves still stand the test of time.

As well as changing the name of Juniper Hill to Lark Rise, Flora Thompson (Flora Timms before her marriage) changed her own name in the books to Laura Timmins and that of her younger brother Edwin to Edmund, but the books are effectively autobiographical. Flora, though very much of the hamlet, was also slightly detached from it. It is probably significant that her father, although not much better off than anyone else, was not an agricultural labourer: he was a stonemason working in Brackley, had come from outside the area and he was also something of a radical in his political leanings. Flora Thompson brings this detachment to bear when, writing when she was in her sixties, she depicts the lost world of her childhood. It would be wrong to describe the books as nostalgic, but there is certainly an elegiac note to them. She is depicting a way of life at the point where it was in the throes of disappearing: "All times are times of transition; but the eighteen-eighties were so in a special sense, for the world was at the beginning of a new era... even to simple country people the change was apparent," she writes.

Lark Rise does not brush away the hardness of life in the hamlet: "'Poverty's no disgrace, but 'tis a great inconvenience' was a common saying among the Lark Rise people; but that puts the case too mildly, for their poverty was no less than a hampering drag upon them," Flora writes. There was indeed great poverty in Juniper Hill. Despite the best efforts of Joseph Arch, George Mitchell and those like them to organise an agricultural trade union, the plight of the agricultural labourers had hardly improved between the early

1870s and the decade which followed: the standard wage paid by the farmer who held the one and only farm in the Juniper Hill community when Flora was growing up was ten shillings a week. The burden of managing a household on such a pitiful income fell primarily on the wives, as Flora makes clear. *Lark Rise* may not be overtly feminist, but it certainly is imbued with a great understanding of and sympathy for the lot of rural women at that time.

Flora Thompson is honest in her portrayal of class in the countryside, too: "the gentry flitted across the scene like kingfishers crossing a flock of hedgerow sparrows" is the striking simile she uses at one point. As for the rector, like many Anglican clergymen of the time he is portrayed as a stout upholder of the status-quo. As he tells Laura/Flora and the other children in the local primary school, "God had placed them just where they were in the social order and given them their own especial work to do; to envy others or to try to change their own lot in life was a sin of which he hoped they would never be guilty".

But *Lark Rise* is not a political critique of late nineteenth century agricultural England. Flora Thompson's success comes from her ability to empathise with the individual characters of Lark Rise, people like Old Sally and Queenie whose memories went back to an earlier time in the hamlet, the men working the fields, the tramps calling at the front doors for food or the occasional travelling salesman looking to sell household goods to an impoverished community. Flora Thompson's books provide a record of the Oxfordshire dialect of her childhood, the children's playground games and rhymes, and the popular songs (including the one or two remaining traditional folk ballads) sang by the men in the Wagon and Horses. Above all, though, *Lark Rise* celebrates the basic humanity of those who lived their lives in Juniper Hill.

As she puts it, "The men's incomes were the same to a penny; their circumstances, pleasures, and their daily field work were shared in common; but in themselves they differed, as other men of their day differed in country and town. Some were intelligent, others slow at the uptake; some were kind and helpful, others selfish; some vivacious, others taciturn. If a stranger had gone there looking for the conventional Hodge, he would not have found him."

Flora Thompson's own life trajectory took her away from Juniper Hill and the north Oxfordshire countryside to live with her husband variously in Bournemouth, east Hampshire and Devon. Others from her family emigrated to Australia. Her brother Edwin travelled the world before being killed in the First World War. It was, as she said in *Lark Rise*, a time of transition. Cities and towns were filling up as the countryside emptied. Hodge – to use the pejorative stereotype one last time – was leaving the land.

But of course the relationship between the city and the countryside remains today a complex one. Cities are seen as representing a form of civilisation, a place of economic power, political power, culture, education and all that is best about cosmopolitanism. The countryside can be seen as backward and out of touch. But then cities can also be depicted as urban jungles, dirty, noisy, places of frantic busyness in money-making while the countryside can be viewed as quiet and beautiful, the repository of the simple and perhaps more genuine way of living. (The BBC's series *Escape to the Country*, which feeds on urban-dwellers' projected vision of the countryside, was first broadcast in 2002 and is still going strong as I write this fifteen years later.)

Juniper Hill today hardly goes out of its way to attract tourists. There's no teashop or Flora Thompson Heritage Centre, something which is probably a blessing. The sparsely-furnished labourers' cottages Flora Thompson depicted in *Lark Rise*, with their privies out in the back gardens, have either been demolished or turned into decent twenty-first century homes. There was one for sale when I was there, a three bedroom cottage selling at around £400,000; the estate agents' sales particulars were stressing the good road and rail connections. Lark Rise has gone for ever and Juniper Hill today is, I think, a hamlet mainly for commuters.

Helmdon

Northamptonshire is a curiously shaped county, with plenty of north-east to offer but no north-west at all, plenty of south-west but no south-east. It's a wedge between the Midlands and the Home Counties.

I entered the county at its bottom left hand corner at Brackley and my route meant that – after a couple of days – I would be leaving it at the top right to enter into Lincolnshire. Compared with the approach from Juniper Hill, the roads leaving Brackley northwards were a pleasure. I found quiet lanes once again and the miles quickly disappeared. And as I cycled, one by one the main transport arteries between London and the Midlands and North arrived and were left behind.

Just north of Towcester I encountered Watling Street, the Roman road which ran from Dover via London to Wroxeter and which in its modern guise as the A5 carries on through Shropshire and north Wales to Holyhead. A little beyond Watling Street, I came across the Grand Union canal at the village of Stoke Bruerne. One of the pubs close to the Canal and River Trust's Canal Museum there temptingly offered special prices on pints for Morris dancers, but I didn't have the right clothes on and anyway it was too early for drinking.

Beyond Stoke Bruerne near the village of Ashton I cycled under the main West Coast railway line from Euston and only a few miles further picked up the sound of the rumble of traffic on the M1. A small roadbridge took me over the motorway into the heart of Salcey Forest, a remnant of mediaeval hunting forest which is now managed by the Forestry Commission and is a popular destination for walkers.

I was conscious, though, that if I were to retrace my route in the years to come, I would probably encounter another major transport link cutting its way through this part of Northamptonshire: the route of the HS2 rail link from London to Birmingham is due to come through a little to the east of

Brackley. The town will not, of course, get a new railway station and there had been, I gathered, some local opposition to the HS2 plans although I can't say the objectors were very visible when I was there.

I was thinking of HS2, however, when I found myself entering the village of Helmdon, a few miles north of Brackley. As I had cycled up from Dorset I'd encountered several times the legacy in the landscape of old branch railway lines. I had passed over and under small derelict railway bridges and noticed the occasional overgrown embankment or cutting. But what I cycled over at the approaches to Helmdon was different: an abandoned railway, certainly, but one built on a grand scale. This was not a rural branch line which during its heyday had seen small steam engines puffing along with a carriage or two behind: this was a railway that, once upon a time, had been built to impress.

What I had stumbled on, I realised, was the remains of the Great Central Railway, the last mainline rail connection to be built between London and the North – and the only main line to London to have suffered the ignominy of closure in the Beeching era. The Great Central was built long after the other major railway companies had built their lines. Its opening celebrations held in London in 1899 were more than half a century after the railway mania of the 1840s had created the core framework of England's railway network and more than thirty years after the last great London terminus at St Pancras had been constructed. The Great Central's London terminus where the celebratory banquet was held was Marylebone, not precisely one of the capital's prestige railway destinations. You might ask whether the £6.5m spent to get the Great Central to London was a sensible investment.

There were those, even at the time of the opening day events, who asked this too. One of the guest speakers, the Cabinet Minister Charles Ritchie MP, voiced the unspoken worries: "he had no doubt that the question which had often been anxiously asked by those responsible for the making and administration of that line had been, was there room for another line into London?" reads the report of his speech. He went on with rather less than full enthusiasm to add, "Those who were responsible for that line were justified in believing that the time had arrived when they might with confidence seek that entrance into London".

Those who were responsible were the directors of what had previously been the Manchester, Sheffield and Lincolnshire Railway until it changed its name in 1897. The attraction of extending their business southwards through Nottingham, Leicester and Rugby was in large measure the opportunity to service the coal mining areas and to bring coal and other minerals to the capital. The company did a deal with the Metropolitan Line, which ran out from Baker Street into Hertfordshire and Buckinghamshire, to use Metropolitan tracks for the route into London although the Great Central later managed to fall out with the Metropolitan and then had to strike a separate deal with the Great Western Railway as well. All in all, you can understand Charles Ritchie's caution.

Nevertheless you have to be impressed at the speed at which the Victorians made things happen. The necessary Parliamentary approval for the line was finally obtained in 1892, and the first spade went in the ground in 1894. There were all sorts of problems. In Nottingham the railway works broke through into the basement strongroom of a bank and the company had to buy the building and rehouse the bank. In Leicester, several streets of houses 'of the poorer class' were destroyed and hundreds of cottages had to be built to replace them. In Brackley, an impressive 20-arch viaduct just to the east of the town was originally supposed to have had 22 arches before a landslip compelled the contractors to change the plans and erect two girder spans instead. Three and a half million cubic yards of earth were removed just on the section of construction through Northamptonshire and Buckinghamshire to the Metropolitan line. 100,000 cubic yards of brickwork were used. You get the general idea.

In a few short years the landscape along the line of the Great Central was transformed in a way which today can seem extraordinary. We seem to have lost the will when it comes to being prepared to welcome the kinds of radical change to the countryside of the kind the Victorians went in for. What's more, when the country does decide to undertake big construction projects – as it seems to have done with HS2 – the speed at which things progress is a fraction of that which would have been the norm in the nineteenth century.

Perhaps it's good that there are now much stricter planning controls and procedures in place to rein in over-enthusiastic capitalist enterprises, the modern equivalents of the Great Central. Or perhaps we have become frightened of change. Perhaps we want the countryside unchanged and unchanging, to reassure us that something in a fast-moving world is constant.

Wellingborough

Jacqui Norton had one place on the outskirts of Wellingborough that she was insistent I should visit. It was a bleak area of rough ground out to the north-west of the town centre, beyond a modern industrial estate, and when she and I visited it we couldn't get any further than a road which ran along its northern boundary. The land itself was firmly fenced off with signs warning of security guards. Beyond the fences I could see heavy earth-moving equipment. This patch of land will shortly become – perhaps by now it has already become – another large industrial park. The brochure I downloaded later on the internet told me that over 150,000 square metres of warehousing were being created by the developers. 'Wellingborough West' is the name they are giving to the new estate.

But this, Jacqui told me, is the land known historically as Bareshanks. She showed me an old map which gave the names of the fields hereabouts and there, sure enough, on the map were exactly the same shapes to the field boundaries as I could see on the ground in front of me: as Jacqui had said, the map showed me that this land had once been called Bareshanks. And this, she went on, was common land where in the Spring of 1650 an event in Wellingborough's history took place.

A very memorable event, Jacqui would want to argue, so much so that she has been encouraging the developers of the industrial estate to put a small heritage board among the new warehouses to commemorate the event. What's more, she has also for the past seven years or so been the prime mover in organising an annual community festival in Wellingborough which remembers and celebrates this history. And yet, as the name of her festival makes clear, the Wellingborough Diggers' Festival appears superficially to be about a very prosaic and workaday event. What happened in 1650 was that a group of local people went to Bareshanks and began to dig up the ground. It's what happens nowadays up and down the country in back gardens and allotments every weekend. A heritage board to remember a group of diggers? Why?

The reason, as Jacqui Norton was happy to explain to me, is because the Wellingborough Diggers, and the other groups of men and women who were given the name of 'Diggers' at this time, were doing more than just taking their spades to the land and sowing seeds. They were, in their way, trying to change society in a very radical way.

I mentioned briefly Thomas Hobbes' work of political philosophy *Leviathan* when I visited his home town of Malmesbury, and I added that it was first published in 1651. It is time to return once more to that period of English history, the years when the country was a republic. In January 1649, let me remind you, the House of Commons resolved to put King Charles on trial for high treason, pronouncing that the sovereign power in the country came from 'the People' rather than from the monarch. The Commons' decision followed the battles and skirmishes of the Royalist revolt the year before, when King Charles had unwisely unleashed a second Civil War and when many of those in the Commons who had previously tried to negotiate a compromise settlement with him finally realised this would not be possible. At the end of January Charles was convicted; three days later, on January 30th 1649, he was executed. In March the Commons formally abolished the office of the monarchy and for good measure also abolished the House of Lords. Later that Spring the country was declared to be a Commonwealth.

This period of our history, referred to by many historians as the English Revolution, was no doubt for some people a time of fear, confusion and loss. But for others it was, as revolutionary times always are, a heady period when everything was up for discussion, when old ways of doing things were being challenged and when there were hopes and dreams of bringing about a better way of organising human society. What happened at Bareshanks reflected this. The Wellingborough Diggers were part of the ferment of the time, and for them the answer lay in direct action – the act of taking over the uncultivated waste ground on the edge of the town and by their own efforts trying to make the land fruitful.

The Declaration which they wrote and published in 1650 has survived and is safely looked after these days in the British Library, but I found it rather more easily online on one of the local websites which publicise Jacqui's festival. It begins in this way: "A Declaration of the Grounds and Reasons why we the Poor Inhabitants of the Town of Wellinborrow, in the

County of Northampton, have begun and give consent to dig up, manure and sow Corn upon the Common and waste ground called Bareshanks, belonging to the Inhabitants of Wellinborrow."

There were good practical reasons to try to grow food on uncultivated land. In Wellingborough, the Diggers' Declaration went on to say, there were over 1100 people who were in need of financial support from the parish. "We have spent all we have, our trading is decayed, our wives and children cry for bread, our lives are a burden to us, divers of us having 5,6,7,8,9 in Family, and we cannot get bread for one of them by our labor." There was little help on offer from others: "Rich men's hearts are hardened, they will not give us if we beg at their doors". There was an immediate attractiveness, in other words, in the do-it-yourself remedy being tried out at Bareshanks.

Wellingborough was by no means exceptional in terms of the general distress being felt in the country at large. The period from 1620 had been one of extreme hardship for many, and the civil wars between Parliamentary forces and the Royalists (the first civil war of 1642-1646, and the second of 1648) had exacerbated things, as armies criss-crossed the country simply taking what they needed. The 1648 harvest had been an exceptionally poor one and the weather during the winter of 1648-1649 was tough. More generally, the population of the country had grown rapidly in the sixteenth and early seventeenth centuries so that even in good years the country did not grow all the corn it needed, grain for bread having to be imported from elsewhere in Europe.

At the same time, however, large areas of potentially productive farmland were not being cultivated: one estimate at the time was that a third of the land area was being left as barren waste. So, although the act of digging up the common land was not one sanctioned by law, the Wellingborough Diggers seem to have been able to enjoy at least some local support: their Declaration mentions the support they have received from three local 'rich men' with commoners' rights. It also adds that a number of 'country farmers' had donated to the Diggers the seed they needed to sow.

However, the Wellingborough Diggers were motivated not just by reasons of practical necessity. This was, after all, a time of revolution. Their Declaration sets out the view that they held on the way more generally that the land should be used and owned: "We find in the Word of God, that God made the Earth for the use and comfort of all Mankind, and let him in it to till and dresse it...". The key phrase here is 'all Mankind': the land, the Diggers argued, was for all to enjoy. They went on to criticise those who held the land for private gain, again using the Bible to support their argument: "Also we find, that God never gave it to any sort of people, that they should have it all to themselves, and shut out all the rest".

The Wellingborough Digger colony was one of several which were established in 1649 and early 1650 in areas of southern England and the south Midlands, of which the most well-known is the one which began in March 1649 on St George's Hill in Weybridge, Surrey. The story of the Diggers of 'George Hill', and in particular their leader Gerrard Winstanley, was almost completely forgotten for more than two centuries before being rediscovered by historians at the end of the nineteenth century. Today the Diggers have become a source of inspiration for many: for community activists such as Jacqui Norton in Wellingborough, for environmentalists, for those campaigning around food politics, and indeed for many others who are seeking a new, more collective, form of politics. The song *The World Turned Upside Down*, written about the Diggers some years back by the singer-songwriter Leon Rosselson, has become something of an anthem for those who wish to celebrate this episode of English history. It includes the verse:

We come in peace, they said, to dig and sow
We come to work the lands in common and
    to make the waste ground grow
This earth divided we will make whole
So it will be a common treasury for all.

Leon Rosselson is borrowing here directly from the language of Gerrard Winstanley. Winstanley wrote what was effectively the Diggers' manifesto *The True Levellers Standard Advanced* which was published in April 1649 and which seeks to explain the Diggers' philosophy: "The work we are going about is this, to dig up George Hill and the waste ground thereabouts and to sow corn, and to eat our bread together by the sweat of our brows. And the first reason is this, that we may work in righteousness and lay the foundation of making the earth a common treasury for all, both rich and poor, that everyone that is born in the land may be fed by the earth his mother that brought him forth… Not enclosing any part into any particular hand, but all as one man working together and feeding together as sons of one father, members of one family."

Winstanley returned again and again in his writings to the theme of the land as common treasury: "The poorest man hath as true a title and just right to the land as the richest man," he wrote later.

While the act of digging on common land could be seen, therefore, as a tactic justified by need and hunger, the Diggers' underlying beliefs were far more threatening to the status-quo. They were effectively asking the question of who should own the land.

And therefore, perhaps not surprisingly, they were seen as a threat which had to be removed. The different Digger communities suffered considerable harassment and oppression. Winstanley and his fellow colonists at St George's Hill in Surrey saw their crops destroyed and the houses they had erected pulled down and burned. Legal action was taken against them. Cattle at Winstanley's nearby farmstead were seized by bailiffs. The Diggers retreated from St George's Hill to nearby Cobham and continued with their efforts to grow crops for a few further months before dispersing. And afterwards? St George's Hill remained open land for several more centuries but was eventually acquired by a developer and it has now become one of the most exclusive private estates in the country: around 420 houses are looked after twenty-four hours a day by security guards behind private gates and their occupants have their own golf course and private tennis courts to enjoy. It is not quite Winstanley's common treasury for all.

In Wellingborough, things were even more short-lived. Here, too, the Diggers came up against the law. "Let those men be effectually proceeded against at the next Sessions," a Northamptonshire Justice of the Peace was instructed in a report from the Council of State. Four Diggers were arrested, the rest sent on their way. Bareshanks became bare again.

But ideas can perhaps be more difficult to banish than people. Over the centuries since 1649 and 1650 the 'land question' has periodically resurfaced in our country's political life, and since the way that the English landscape looks depends on the way that the land is owned and worked, this may be the moment to take stock of how this particular story has unfolded.

After all, when you think about it, there is something fundamentally curious about the idea that the land on the earth's surface, the underlying rocks which make up our planet and the soil that covers them, can in some sense be legally in the possession of individuals. How did we as humans come up with an idea which might seem to a visiting hitchhiker from elsewhere in the galaxy a very curious way of doing things?

In fact, according to Andro Linklater whose 2014 book *Owning the*

Earth explores exactly this question, different human societies have taken different approaches. "Across the globe people have evolved a myriad means of owning the places they live in," he writes. But he is particularly interested in looking at the development of the model of private individualised ownership, and to do this he looks at the evolution of land ownership in Britain from mediaeval times onwards and the way the British model was exported to the lands of the New World in North America. It is in one sense, he says, a 'monstrous method of owning the earth', requiring constant justification and legal back-up. On the other hand, he points out, it had the effect in Britain of monetarising land and of creating a class of asset which could then be used to kick-start the industrial revolution. The idea of individual ownership of land has proved to be, he suggests, both "the most destructive and creative cultural force in written history".

It is a model that has not always been without vocal critics. Let's start the story more than two hundred and fifty years after the Diggers, in the first decade of the twentieth century. More precisely let's start in November 1909 when David Lloyd George introduced in his Budget a proposal for a series of taxes on land values. His so-called People's Budget incurred the immediate wrath of the House of Lords (whose members, after all, were those most affected by the proposal) and the Lords rejected it. The country plunged into one of the most serious constitutional crises in modern times and only after an emergency General Election and further lengthy wrangling in Parliament was the Commons' supremacy on Budgetary matters confirmed.

Lloyd George had joked at the time that a Duke cost as much for the country to keep as two battleships and he had used rhetoric at a public meeting in Newcastle just before his Budget which wouldn't have been unfamiliar to Gerrard Winstanley: "Who made ten thousand men the owners of the soil and the rest of us trespassers in the land of our birth?" he asked. Lloyd George's choice of statistic could have been open to challenge, but nevertheless it was indeed the case that the great bulk of the land in Britain was in the hands of relatively few landowners. A survey of land ownership, sometimes described as the second Domesday Book, had taken place in 1872 and had reported that 400 peers and peeresses owned between them almost six million acres and that a further 1300 great landowners held an additional 8.5 million acres.

The decision by Parliament to compile the 1872 Return of Owners of Land was something of an own-goal for the landowning classes, and the potentially embarrassing information it contained was hurriedly buried. The journalist Kevin Cahill who tried to identify modern-day land ownership for his 2001 book *Who Owns Britain* called the 1872 Return "our lost book", claiming that it had been hidden away successfully for over a century deep in record offices. Today, he says, finding out the information which was publicly available in 1872 is altogether more difficult although the headline claim in his book is the striking one that 189,000 families hold forty million of the UK's sixty million acres.

Lloyd George's attempt to introduce taxation on land followed a lengthy period when the 'land issue' was a focal point in politics: 'an important, even a burning issue', according to one historian. There were active pressure groups, such as the Land Nationalisation Society (established in 1881) and the English Land Restoration League (set up in 1883, as the Land Reform Union), both of which sent out speakers to the countryside to undertake propaganda work. The LNS's 'yellow vans' and the ELRL's 'red vans', horse-drawn of course, were a familiar sight on village greens during the 1890s. Both organisations drew inspiration from the American writer Henry George, whose book *Progress and Poverty* (1879) was particularly focused on the idea of land value taxation: don't kick out the landlords, Henry George once said, tax them out instead.

There was a particular logic in the nineteenth century and early twentieth century for examining the issue of land value because the rapid urbanisation of Britain's cities and towns had led to astonishingly high windfall returns for those individual landowners who happened to hold the land required for the new houses. The country as a whole needed the new homes, the argument went, so why should the increased value of the land not be shared by all?

It will be seen that there was a difference of tactics between those advocating a 'common treasury'-type approach to the country's land (where the logic suggested common ownership) and those who weren't necessarily so concerned about the legal ownership but did want the economic value of land captured for the common good. But in practice the two ideas tended to merge. You can trace both strands back well before Henry George. Those Chartist colonists who moved into their new homes at Charterville may well have debated the issue when they met up socially in the School House (one of the Chartists' national leaders Bronterre O'Brien had called for the 'appropriation of the whole soil of the country to the whole people of the country', for example). The question of the land was debated in the eighteenth century as well. The Newcastle-born radical Thomas Spence, who was born in 1750, advocated common ownership of the land, although his preferred solution was not state ownership through nationalisation but rather parish ownership. What's the word for this, I wonder? Parishisation?

Perhaps what happened at Bareshanks in Wellingborough in 1650 and the role that the Diggers played for a few short months during the English Revolution does after all have its place in our country's history, therefore. But as I got my road map out to try to find the quietest possible route out of Wellingborough northwards towards Kettering, I pondered how this long political debate seems now so completely forgotten. Not in Scotland, of course, where land reform remains a major political issue, but certainly in England. All that debate, all those arguments, all the books written, all the proselytising for land reform… it all seems today to have led to complete political silence.

I mentioned earlier Kevin Cahill's 2001 book on land ownership today. His work, researched with considerable difficulty, was intended as something of a call to arms. "It is increasingly clear that the question the democracy should be asking a lot more forcibly is, 'Who Does Own Britain?'," he wrote. But despite his efforts, it's not.

Corby

North Northamptonshire is the Cotswolds all over again, although without quite the same numbers of visitors.

Oundle luxuriates in warm Jurassic limestone. The town buffs up its houses and cottages to show off the beauty of the local stone to the full, and why not: if you have it flaunt it, and Oundle certainly has it. 'Comforting cosiness in three dimensions' is how one journalist described this old market town in an article I came across, and I know what he meant.

I noticed a café in the heart of the town's centre just as I was about to cycle past, and stopped for a coffee (I may not have mentioned my coffee stops for a while, but believe me, they continued to be a necessary part of my journey). It was a pleasant morning, and there were seats and a few tables outside on the pavement. I took the coffee outside and made the most of continental café culture, Northamptonshire style.

I had a route decision to make. I could divert a little to the village of Fotheringhay to see for myself the site of the castle where Elizabeth I imprisoned her cousin Mary, Queen of Scots. The castle has gone but Fotheringhay, I knew, does have a spectacularly impressive parish church dating back to the early fifteenth century. (Folkies will know that the village and its castle gave their name to the band which Sandy Denny set up in 1970 when she left Fairport Convention, although Sandy Denny managed in the process to mis-spell the name as Fotheringay).

My other route choice lay directly north, to the villages of Woodnewton, Apethorpe and King's Cliffe, and this is the way that in the end I went. I was able to enjoy all the way more examples of Jurassic limestone. Apethorpe in particular was a delight: a beautiful stone village which huddles around a truly gorgeous Jacobean building, classified as Grade I. Apethorpe Palace, once upon a time a favourite residence of King James I, was a building at serious risk of collapse which the government stepped in to compulsorily purchase it in 2004. The state promptly passed it on to English Heritage, who probably wondered how on earth they could find the funds to stop the roof collapsing and taking the intricate Jacobean plaster ceiling work down with it. What happened was that they in turn sold Apethorpe to a private individual, albeit one who was prepared to spend many millions on doing it up and was prepared also to continue to allow public access. His name is Jean Christophe Iseux, Baron von Pfetten, who was born in France in 1969 but is clearly as citizen of the world since as well as being an academic and a diplomat he has also been an advisor to the Chinese government (according to the press, he was brought in to organise back-room negotiations with Iran about its nuclear programme). This is a man with a good contact book, and – it would seem – a good CV when it comes to doing up old buildings. The press release from English Heritage when they sold Apethorpe to the Baron in 2015 included the necessary quote from him: "My wife and I learnt a lot from the ten years we have spent renovating our 17th century chateau in France…Luckily we are young and we have many friends with similar interests keen to support us." And luckily he has money. Still, if you do have millions available to invest in property, I'd suggest Apethorpe Palace is a rather better aesthetic choice for your money than buying into the gated community at St George's Hill.

So there was much to enjoy about the English countryside as I made my way through north Northamptonshire. But before Apethorpe, before my coffee in Oundle, I'd been to Corby.

I do appreciate that conventionally travel books and guide books have places that they visit and places that they don't visit, and that almost certainly Corby is considered to be in the latter category. It's a working-class town, one based on industry. Indeed, Corby exists because there was work to be had in the steelworks at its heart – until, that is, the steelworks closed down and Corby had to start all over again. You don't go to Corby for Jurassic limestone: the architecture of the shopping centre is predominantly post-war concrete.

But nevertheless I wanted to include Corby in my journey. Corby offers a study in landscape too, even if what you get is a particular type of urban landscape. And of course Corby (little more than a village until the 1930s) is what it is today because of the underlying geology – it was the Jurassic ironstone which brought the original steelworks here in the first place.

Corby was a New Town, with capital letters. Every town and village in one sense has been a new town at some point in its past, but Corby was one of the official new towns set up under the post-war Labour government's

New Towns Act of 1946. It's perhaps hard to remember now just what high hopes accompanied the passing of the Act, which was supported not only by the government but also by the opposition (only one Conservative spoke against it). There was a desperate need for housing, with many working-class areas of London and other major cities having suffered particularly bad bombing damage during the war. The houses which remained unbombed, many of them at least, were jerry-built and barely fit for human habitation. The answer was to start again: relocate people from the inner-cities to new, properly designed housing in properly designed, planned, communities. Lewis Silkin, the Minister of Town and Country Planning, who presented the New Towns Bill to Parliament saw the new town dream as doing more than offering houses. "We may well produce in the new towns a new type of citizen, a healthy, self-respecting dignified person with a sense of beauty, culture and civic pride," he said.

Citizens with a sense of beauty: new towns were not just to be utilitarian dormitories. Art, for example, shouldn't only be something enjoyed by the well-off: the new towns would be given outdoor sculptures and other public artworks. (Another new town, Harlow, had a Henry Moore sculpture outside its shopping centre.) Perhaps there was an element of top-down paternalism in all this; perhaps there was the idea that, if you gave people lovely new places to live in they'd turn into lovely new human beings. But it's hard to fault the desire to make people's lives better.

Corby was the last of a first wave of new towns which followed the passing of the 1946 Act, coming along after places like Harlow, Stevenage, Crawley, Basildon and Peterlee, and before 1960s- and 1970s- new towns such as Telford, Skelmersdale and of course Milton Keynes. Corby was designated a new town in 1950 mainly because the alternative was to let it continue as the single company town it had effectively become when the steelworks had been built in 1934. As a new town, Corby could – it was hoped – diversify its employment. It could get a proper town centre, too.

That original shopping centre is still there more than half a century later. For students of fifties architecture it's a must-see, with its segregated traffic, pedestrianised streets and two-deck shopping. For the rest of us, well, let's just say nothing more than that it's rather showing its age. Corby didn't appear to strike lucky in terms of getting any Henry Moores, but what I did see in the town centre were clocks: big futuristic 1950s-style outdoor clocks, fit to tell the time for the better days ahead.

Corby was an anomaly in north Northamptonshire, and it has always been a place which has attracted incoming migrants. It's particularly well known for its large Scottish community; look out for Scotch pies in the bakers' shops, I was told. Irn Bru sells well of course. A saltire flag (admittedly rather torn, with the blue of the St Andrew's cross rather faded) was hanging from one of the flats above the shops, and there is still a bus service each day which starts in Corby and takes you direct to Glasgow. Corby has also long attracted residents from further afield, particularly from eastern Europe: a Serbian orthodox church has been a feature in the town for very many years, for example.

Tom Beattie arrived in Corby with his family when he was a sixteen-year old. His accent reveals that he is not part of the Scottish diaspora, but rather that his family originally came from Belfast (there are sizeable Irish and Welsh communities too in the town). "I came here in 1972, having grown up in a traditional working-class city, close to the shipyards. Corby was a very different place. It all looked a bit odd to me," he tells me. But there was something still of a pioneering spirit about the place. "People who came here did so as a result of making a choice: they wanted to improve their lives," he adds.

Tom's working life (he was a trade union official) took him away from Corby but he has now returned and a few years ago took over as the district council's Leader. He leads a council which is solidly Labour in a mainly rural constituency which has a Conservative MP. I met him in his office in the council offices, a bright new building called the Cube which also hosts a theatre and arts venue and the main public library. I wanted to know what he and his colleagues have planned for the next phase of Corby's life.

Human settlements spring up where there is work to be had so the closure of what was the big employer in Corby, British Steel's works, at the very start of the 1980s was a very heavy blow for the town. Corby embarked on a downward spiral, Tom Beattie tells me. It needed new jobs, jobs with companies who were prepared to make their home in Corby and weren't just there in the short-term to mop up the various grants and incentives which the government made available (there were plenty of the latter sort of company). Corby needed regeneration.

It still does, although Tom says that the town has weathered the storm. "The image of Corby has altered significantly. Before, the attitude was 'everybody hates us, we don't care'. Now people are proud of Corby," he says. That is, of course, exactly what you'd expect the leader of a council to tell a passing journalist, but I was prepared to give him the benefit of the doubt. A modern indoor shopping arcade, Willow Place, has recently been built next to the 1950s shops. There's a 50 metre indoor swimming pool. There's the reopened railway station with direct trains to London. There's the Cube itself, which admittedly almost caused financial meltdown for the council when it was being built, but at least *was* built and is now being used, hopefully delivering all that culture and civic pride that Lewis Silkin had in mind.

But there is only so much a local authority can do. Tom and I look out of the windows of his office across to some of the tired post-war architecture opposite. Surely he must be thinking of redeveloping that part of the town? "Our town centre is privately owned. Most people don't understand that," he replies. "It was sold off, and has been in different hands, and a private company has it now. That frustrates me, because we can't do things we'd like to do," he says.

In fact, the issue of land ownership very rapidly led to the end of that original 1946 cross-party consensus in Parliament on new towns. Labour's view was the freehold of the land in places like Corby should be collectively held, being passed after the development phase to the relevant local authority. The Conservatives resolved in 1959 that new town assets would be held in a national public body rather than locally and then after 1979 instituted the policy which saw the new towns' commercial and industrial assets sold off to private buyers. Regeneration these days requires partnership working: Corby council works with the private sector and with government agencies to try to make things happen.

The secret for a stronger Corby in the future, according to Tom Beattie, is for more housing. The town needs to grow rather than contract, he says, and the population, which was about 50,000 at the beginning of this century, is targeted under the council's current development strategy to become 100,000 by 2030. "The ambition is to double our population. We are already the fastest growing area outside London," Tom explains. The countryside is attractive, the housing is affordable, and London is not too far away. We need new homes here, he says. And he goes on to suggest that the old idea, that the local authority can be the provider of decent housing, should be brought back. "I want to see council housing," he says. "When did people stop talking about council housing?"

Something has certainly changed in the years since the New Towns Act of 1946, and not just in relation to housing provision. Back then the country seemed to relish the idea of the new, the bold, the modern; now we are keen to preserve things, at almost any cost. Heritage is the watchword.

And yet if Lewis Silkin's paternalist but enlightened post-war idea of new towns is out of fashion, the ideas associated with an earlier twentieth century experiment in creating new communities are still very much in vogue. Ebenezer Howard's visionary idea for Garden Cities, spelled out originally in his 1898 book *To-morrow, A peaceful path to real reform,* was for garden cities to bring together the best of urban and country life. Garden cities would have pure air and water, direct access to natural beauty, low rents and rates, an absence of slums but plenty of opportunity for good quality social and community life.

The garden city ideal was very influential, and not just in places like Letchworth and Welwyn Garden City where Howard's ideas were actually tried out in practice. You could say that the English desire for sprawling suburban areas of cities, with semi-detached or detached houses set in their own gardens, was a somewhat corrupted version of Howard's original vision. Other countries went for high-density urban living; we moved out to the leafy suburbs.

There's a tension under all this talk of planned new towns between our human urge to have things properly planned and our equally human love of things being a bit higgledy-piggledy and untidy. Whatever the original intentions of those who helped create our new towns, places change, people live their lives where they find themselves, and new generations come along.

But sometimes, long afterwards, we find ourselves really rather fond of what were once new towns. Remember Northleach with its carefully measured burgage plots? Remember Stow-on-the-Wold?

Collyweston

If you are a geologist there are certain English place names which are very familiar to you, even if you've never been anywhere near the places themselves. Collyweston is one of these names. W. J. Arkell includes a section on Collyweston Oolite in his magisterial 1933 book on Jurassic geology, a classic text, so I knew that I needed to steer my bicycle in the direction of the village. Fortunately it was very much on my route.

What was brought out of the ground here a few miles south of Stamford were stone slates, similar to the Stonesfield slates which I saw Julian Palmer and his workers extracting from the Tinker's Barn quarry near Naunton. The geological difference is that, while the Stonesfield slates come from Great Oolite strata, at Collyweston the slates are Inferior Oolite, from earlier in the Jurassic period. But what Stonesfield and Collyweston slates have in common is that they are both ideal for roofing purposes.

The heyday of the Collyweston slate industry was in the eighteenth and nineteenth centuries, when large numbers of people made their living from the quarrying. It was not easy work. Originally the slates had been able to be taken directly from the ground but, as the easily accessed stone became worked out, it became necessary to go underground. Shafts thirty or forty feet down were built to access the stone beds. Miners crouched or lay in the shafts for ten or twelve hours a day, digging out the sand and soft earth below the slates until the 'logs' of stone fell away and could be brought to the surface.

To turn the 'logs' into slates for roofing required splitting the stone, and for this the quarrymen relied on the weather. The most important time for the Collyweston pits were the winter months when there was the strong chance of frosts. The extracted stone on the surface was kept well-watered during this time, ready for cold days and nights when the water would freeze and expand, naturally splitting the stone into the slates required. Somebody had the job of keeping the piles of stones suitably damp all the time, and if by ill-chance the weather one winter was too mild to complete the work the remaining stones were buried in a deep pit covered with wet earth and left until the frosts of the following winter.

You can still find people selling Collyweston slates today although mining effectively ceased in the early 1960s. The village has changed enormously since then and the old ways have almost been forgotten. I met Sandra Johnson in Collyweston's village shop and she told me a family story of her mother being taken out one night to see Sandra's great-grandfather at work watering the slates. But Sandra is unusual: she was born and brought up in the village and indeed can claim family links with Collyweston going back to the 1500s. When she was younger, most of the villagers worked either in the stone industry or for one of five local farms. "Now people live here and work elsewhere," she says.

She mentions that her next-door neighbour commutes daily to London. I express surprise – we are, after all, in the very northernmost corner of Northamptonshire – but she explains that many people from the village drive their cars to Peterborough to catch the fast trains south, while others go to nearby Stamford to catch trains to places like Cambridge. It does affect village life a little when everyone is out at work, adds her husband Paul.

Paul and Sandra retired after many years of running a family estate agency business in Stamford and took the decision to move back to Sandra's childhood village, making the move from Stamford to Collyweston in 2004. Much that Sandra remembered from her childhood had gone: "We had a school, a post office, a garage, a butcher's shop, another little shop and three pubs," she says. The school was shut a generation back and slowly almost all the other village services closed as well, with just one of the three pubs Sandra remembers still being open today. Other than the pub, the village has a church and a village hall.

And, since the red-letter day of July 1st 2010, it also has a community shop. It wasn't by accident that I had arranged to meet Paul and Sandra there, for they were instrumental in the work of establishing it and they remain active committee members and volunteers. Collyweston's shop is run for the village's benefit, and indeed is legally registered as a community benefit society. Profits, aside from the reserves which need to be built up for things like replacement chiller cabinets, are passed on as donations to local organisations and societies.

But mostly the shop offers a more intangible benefit to Collyweston. "There's more going on in the village. Now people stop at the shop and have a natter. And we do home deliveries to people who are poorly," Sandra explains. It's also helping people to get to know their neighbours: Paul mentions one couple who are volunteering in the shop who had lived in Collyweston for fifteen years without really making any local friends.

The shop operates with a part-time paid manager Rachel who works mornings five days a week and takes responsibility for ordering the stock, but otherwise relies on locals as volunteers. This can have its own challenges, particularly in the summer months when many people are away on holiday, but Sandra says that without volunteers the business would not be viable. Indeed, the venture went through a wobble in its early days when it operated with a full-time member of staff – and found itself running out of money.

Collyweston's community shop is tiny, with stock crammed into every nook and corner. You can buy wrapping paper and birthday balloons, wild bird mix, specialist artisan pies made just up the road in Rutland, locally brewed beer, meat from a Stamford butchery business, bread from a local bakery and other specialist things which, according to Sandra, you won't find in the big Stamford supermarkets. But of course you can also buy milk and pick up the papers.

The efforts taken by Paul and Sandra and their fellow committee members and volunteers have been recognised with a series of awards. But there is plenty to get right: as Sandra says, we may have a small shop but we still have to deal with sourcing issues, with pricing, with food hygiene, health and safety procedures, and with food waste.

Collyweston, like most community-run village shops and pubs, was helped in its early days with advice from the specialist co-operative agency the Plunkett Foundation and I'd taken the opportunity earlier on my travels to call into their office in Woodstock, just outside the main gate of Blenheim Palace. There, in between the staff desks, was a blackboard on which somebody had chalked in the key information I was after: it told me that there were 344 community-run village shops up and running around the UK. Perhaps the number has since gone up: the blackboard also stated that there were a further 45 potentially on their way, whose committee members were in touch with the Plunkett Foundation and currently getting support.

The roll-call of those 344 shops didn't include perhaps the best-known village-run community shop of them all, the one in the village of Ambridge which – if you listen to The Archers – you will may recall was reopened in 2010 as a volunteer-led venture. The story-line in the Archers was put together with strong input from the Plunkett Foundation, with both scriptwriters and actors at the time taking the trouble to research carefully exactly what a rural English village community would be likely to do. Even today, several years after the Ambridge village shop was saved, the Ambridge storyline helps inspire real-life efforts, Plunkett Foundation staff told me.

Despite the hard work of people like Sandra and Paul Johnson up and down the country, and despite the efforts of those trying to advise them, the loss of village shops is continuing apace. There are no statistics of village shop closures centrally collected by the government, but the Plunkett Foundation estimates that around 400 privately-run stores close each year. I'd noticed along the way the evidence: there was one attractive private house in a village near Juniper Hill, for example, with the nameboard outside reading "The Old Shop". There was a house in Apethorpe which was called "The Old Post Office". These were the villages where you couldn't get a pint of milk or a loaf of bread – or for that matter meet up to have a chat with the neighbours.

Community-run shops can vary enormously with some relying entirely on volunteers and others employing full-time managers but most are registered, as at Collyweston, as community benefit societies. The Plunkett Foundation has sets of model legal rules available and it can also point new groups in the direction of funding sources. Government grant funding to support village shops has currently been withdrawn but there are other lenders and charitable foundations keen to support the idea and, increasingly, village shops are turning to find investment capital from within their own communities through so-called community share issues. But potential new shops also have to steer clear of over-optimism and ensure they have a strong business plan: the Plunkett Foundation has a team of advisers across the country whose role is not only to support embryonic community groups but also to ask the challenging questions.

Ultimately, I gathered from my visit to the Plunkett Foundation, running a community shop isn't really about running a shop at all. It's a means to an end. It's about trying to find an answer to the fundamental question: what sort of places do we want our villages to be like? It's about community-led action to improve people's own communities.

Barnack

One of the problems of using the raw material from the great Jurassic stone belt to build our villages and towns is what gets left behind: the empty holes where the stone has been quarried.

Centuries of quarrying in north Northamptonshire have involved some really significant rearrangements of the original landscape, and perhaps none so more than at the 22 hectares (54 acres) of tumbled ground just outside the village of Barnack which was my destination after Collyweston. This is the land which you'll find on maps marked, rather quaintly, as Hills and Holes (locals tend to know it by the slightly less picturesque but perhaps more accurate name of Hills and Hollows).

The Jurassic limestone quarried here was called Barnack Rag and has been taken out of the ground since the country was part of the Roman Empire (Barnack Rag has been found at the base of the Romans' London Wall and also in the Roman city of Verulamium, now St Albans). The quarrying was continued in mediaeval times. A number of cathedrals and monastic buildings, including Crowland Abbey close by in Lincolnshire and Ramsey Abbey and Sawtry Abbey (both in Cambridgeshire) used Barnack Rag stone. Even more significant was the use of the stone in the building of Peterborough and Ely cathedrals. The Barnack Rag stone was taken out of the quarry on sleds and dragged the half mile or so down to the River Welland, just to the north of the quarry site. Thereafter boats were used to take the stone away using the local network of rivers and canals.

We have rather forgotten just how important waterways once were as a transport link in this part of England. We may however be about to be reminded. The Fens Waterways Link is an ambitious project which, if it finally makes it from the planning stage to reality, will create a series of navigable rivers and canals in this part of eastern England enabling boaters to travel between the cathedral cities of Lincoln, Peterborough and Ely. Market towns such as Spalding, Wisbech and Ramsey will also be linked.

The Fens Waterways Link, which is primarily an Environment Agency project, will potentially create around fifty new miles of navigable rivers and canals to link up with the 145 miles or so of existing navigable waterways in the area. Already work has been undertaken to restore navigation on the Black Sluice Navigation south from Boston but the most dramatic part of the project is the proposal for a new link south between the river Welland (leaving some miles downstream from Barnack) and the river Nene near Peterborough. The Nene is important in this context because it provides access at Northampton to the Grand Union canal and the bulk of the country's canal network. In other words, the Fens Waterways Link could help bring important river- and canal-based tourism to an area of the country which, unlike say the Norfolk Broads, is currently mostly ignored by leisure boaters.

The rejuvenation of the country's canals across Britain in the second half of the twentieth century seems to me a major success story, one which was in many cases very much a bottom-up affair achieved by committed local volunteers. Canals can be hard work – they take a lot of looking after even at the best of times if they are not to leak water or become filled up with silt and debris – but despite all the challenges a large number of canals which had seemed to be gone for ever have been brought back in recent decades into navigable usage. Canals like the Kennet and Avon, the Huddersfield Narrow and the Peak Forest, some of the most popular today with holidaymakers, were among those saved, and efforts are continuing to restore others that today are still derelict. When I had been in the Cotswolds I was aware that I was close to the disused Thames and Severn Canal, now the focus of an active restoration campaign by the Cotswold Canals Trust.

But canal restoration, and proposed new works like the Fens Waterways Link, need serious amounts of money and at a time of austerity funds can be hard to find. Some people in the Fenlands are worried that the Environment Agency is not as committed to the proposed new waterway network as they would like it to be. The reality is that, even when money is available, major infrastructure projects take time – and many of us are impatient for things to happen much more quickly.

If a new waterway link is indeed created between the Welland and Nene rivers it will be too late by many centuries to help transport the Barnack Rag from the Hills and Holes quarries. The mediaeval quarry-workers took away almost every last piece of workable stone. Hills and Holes today, I was told when I visited, is basically just a giant spoil heap.

It is a spoil heap which has, however, discovered an after-life. Hills and Holes is a nationally important site for its flora. Indeed since it was first designated in 1976, this has been officially the Hills and Holes National Nature Reserve, cared for by Natural England. It has also received international endorsement with designation in 2002 as one of the European Union's Special Areas of Conservation. There are orchids growing here: seven or eight species in all, including the Bee Orchid (which really does look as though a bee has landed on the flowers), the Fragrant Orchid and the Twayblade. One of the most unusual orchids is the Man Orchid, so called because (if you are imaginatively minded) each flower can seem to have two 'arms' and two 'legs'. I'm afraid no Man Orchid was prepared to show itself (himself?) to me on the day of my visit, so I can't speak from personal observation.

However if there is one flower which grows here which is the jewel in the reserve's crown it is the very rare Pasque Flower which begins flowering in April, around the time of Easter. The plant is short and hairy, never more than a foot or so in height, and the flowers are a deep purple with bright yellow stamens inside. It is easy to identify, if of course you have been extremely fortunate and managed to find a plant at all: Pasque Flowers are becoming less and less widespread, being restricted currently to a few sites in the Cotswolds, Chilterns and the east of England. At Hills and Holes the Pasque Flower population is carefully monitored from year to year, and at the moment seems to be holding its own.

The orchids and the Pasque Flower are here at Hills and Holes partly because limestone grassland is naturally a botanically rich habitat but also because the ground has been allowed to develop with almost no human intervention ever since the quarries were worked out and left abandoned some six hundred years ago. Nearby land has been used for arable farming, but Hills and Holes presumably seemed just too challenging to be taken into cultivation. It was in 1942 that the site was first extensively subjected to a comprehensive botanical survey, although Hills and Holes has for a very long time been recognised as important for its flora: the first book on wild flowers in Britain *Phytologia Britannica*, which was written by William Howe and was published during the English Commonwealth in 1650, includes three mentions of the site.

The fact that Hills and Holes is a national nature reserve does not mean that the public are not allowed in and indeed Natural England welcomes visitors at the entrances with maps and interpretation boards. Pasque

Flowers and orchids appear to be able to coexist with local dog-walkers and their dogs, and the message of conservation seems to be getting through. I was told that, while in the early days of the reserve there were occasional problems with flower pickers, now the challenge is how to cope when large numbers of photographers descend on the site, keen to get the perfect Pasque Flower portrait. This, I think, counts as progress.

The story of how we decided as a country that looking after flora and fauna is important, and that nature conservation deserves public money spent on it, is one which is particularly associated with the twentieth century. The network of county Wildlife Trusts trace their origins to the creation in 1912 by the banker Charles Rothschild of the Society for the Promotion of Nature Reserves, and to the gifting in 1919 to the Society by Rothschild of an area of wild fenland, Woodwalton Fen. The two-tier idea of national and local nature reserves was formalised as part of the post-war Labour government's extensive legislation on countryside matters, the National Parks and Access to the Countryside Act of 1949. At that stage, national reserves were the responsibility of a new agency Nature Conservancy; over the years this became in turn the Nature Conservancy Council and English Nature. Natural England, the current agency, was created in 2006 (Scotland and Wales now have their own arrangements).

Natural England's work at Hills and Holes includes the employment of a senior reserve manager, who takes responsibility for this and several other nearby nature reserves, who coordinates the volunteer Friends group which helps out at the site, and who oversees the Autumn grazing programme and scrub clearance work which help to protect the grassland areas. That's the hands-on stuff. But Natural England staff also have to sit at desks. The agency has to produce the policy documents and conservation statements which describe how it intends to meet its obligations in looking after an important site. I looked up later on the internet the 'site improvement plan' (SIP) for Hills and Holes which Natural England had produced in 2014. Some of the steps the SIP suggests seem eminently doable. One identified problem, 'nitrogen loading due to high number of dogs using the site', came with the proposed solution 'mitigate nitrogen enrichment through introduction of comprehensive dog waste removal policy to include bins, signs, PR and community engagement'. Get rid of the dog poo, in other words. Natural England assessed the budget implication of this step as being £600, which I suspect it would be able to find, even in straitened times.

Some of Natural England's ideas for Hills and Holes seem altogether more ambitious, however. The SIP's proposed Action 2D, designed to secure the long-term sustainable future for the site, comes in costed at half a million pounds. Natural England talked hopefully in the SIP document of being able to look to raise this through lottery funding and through the European Union's LIFE funding programme which offers support to environmental and nature conservation proposals. EU funding, one has to assume, is no longer going to be much of an option for Hills and Holes.

Much of money needed for Action 2D was designed to secure the ownership of the land at Hills and Holes. It may come as a surprise to some to know that designation as a national nature reserve does not automatically mean that the land is publicly owned. In this case, Natural England are tenants of the site through an agreement with the next-door country estate, centred on the Elizabethan country house Burghley.

Burghley is perhaps not quite as top-notch as Blenheim Palace but it still occupies a major position in the league table of the great aristocratic estates of Britain. The house, constructed in the latter decades of the sixteenth century, comes with thirty-five principal rooms and the lead roof (replaced recently) extends to three quarters of an acre – or at least so the marketing material for Burghley told me. As at Blenheim, Lancelot (Capability) Brown was employed to landscape the parkland at Burghley, and just as he did at Blenheim he decided to sweep away the formal gardens and to construct an artificial lake, the Serpentine Lake.

Burghley has been the seat of the Cecil family for sixteen generations, William Cecil having successfully navigated the political shoals of life at court to be made the first Lord Burghley by Queen Elizabeth in 1571. Later the Cecils became the Earls of Exeter and later still were promoted another rung up the aristocratic ladder to become Marquesses of Exeter. Today's family head, the 8th Marquess ('Michael Exeter' if we are being informal) grew up in Canada and, although he went to Eton and Cambridge University, now lives in the United States, in Oregon. The family member who lives at Burghley is his cousin, Miranda Rock, who looks after the charitable trust which has custody of the house itself. (This is effectively the legal solution introduced by John Hoy at Blenheim; the Exeters set up their charitable trust in 1975.)

The Burghley estate, which extended to 28,000 acres when the second Domesday survey was conducted in the 1870s, continues to own much of this part of England; as well as Hills and Holes, it is the landlord of Collyweston's village shop, for example. This means that Burghley, its Marquesses and their estate managers have been responsible to a quite extraordinary extent in determining how the landscape hereabouts looks.

You could argue that it is thanks to the estate's benign neglect that Hills and Holes has been able over the centuries to become an important wild flower sanctuary. Rather more significantly, it is because of Burghley influence that the town of Stamford, just to the north of here, has developed in the way that it has. Hoskins in *The Making of the English Landscape* devotes several pages to the contrasting development of three Midlands market towns, Stamford, Leicester and Nottingham which as he points out until the later eighteenth century had each followed more or less the same trajectory. Here is Hoskins taking up the story of why Stamford did not become another Nottingham:

> In 1846 there was a good chance that the new main line of railway from London to York would pass through Stamford instead of Peterborough, then a place of no consequence. The people of Stamford were passionately anxious that the railway should come their way, for it was plain enough that the great coaching trade, by which they lived, was doomed. For reasons we need not go into, Lord Exeter successfully prevented the main line from entering the town: it was taken through Peterborough instead. Stamford was killed: in the 1850s its population, which until then had been rising steadily, actually began to fall. There was no housing problem here. The open fields remained open for another generation – until the secret ballot came in 1872, but by then grass was growing in the streets of the town.

Actually Hoskins is quite forthright elsewhere in his book as to Lord Exeter's reasons: until nineteenth century Parliamentary reform, Stamford returned two members of Parliament, and – as Hoskins puts it – "since the end of the seventeenth century the Cecils at Burghley House just outside the town had controlled the election of both members by a combination of methods that seemed to leave no loophole for a mistake". An industrialised or expanded Stamford would have potentially challenged the Cecils' powerbase: the town remained undeveloped. But of course this could today be seen as an advantage. As Hoskins says, Stamford fossilized – and in doing so became a museum piece, "the beautiful seventeenth- and eighteenth-century town we see today".

Land ownership and the English landscape go hand-in-hand: this seems to me incontestable. What can perhaps be contested is the role the big country estates play today. Here, offering one viewpoint, is Miranda Root, the Marquess's cousin, as quoted on the estate's website: "For as long as I can remember, Burghley has filled people with awe and inspiration. Earlier generations of my family have endowed this magical place with beautiful treasures and it is the privilege of all of us who live and work here to share them with you."

Here, offering another perspective, is Raymond Williams, one of the country's most distinguished writers on culture and literature of the last century. Williams is writing from a left-of-centre political position: "I feel the weight of these country houses. Who has not admired the admirable architecture or furniture to be found among them? But if we acknowledge them as a contribution we must also acknowledge them as an obstacle... They are constantly presented to us as 'our heritage', inducing a particular way of seeing and relating to the world... I always see them as profoundly ambivalent."

There are always various ways to interpret the world.

Helpston

I cycled in to the centre of the village of Helpston from Barnack on the B1443 on what I suppose you could describe as the new road. 'New' and 'old' are relative terms, of course, and I don't want you to think that my road has only just been constructed: what I mean is that the main road which today runs through the centre of Helpston is, in landscape terms, a relatively recent arrival. It was laid out the way it is today around the year 1811, two years after a Parliamentary Act had been passed allowing the local landowners to enclose the fields of the parish.

Before enclosure my route to Helpston would have brought me in by a meandering lane to the north of the village and I'd have turned off it to cross the little stream of Rhyne Dyke, crossing the large open common field known as Lolham Bridge Field to get to the church and the heart of the settlement. Today, at the parish boundary, there's an abrupt right-angle bend south on the B1443 and then shortly afterwards another ninety-degree turn eastwards on to a road which gets you straight to the village centre. This road, dead straight and on an almost exact west-east axis, is surrounded by a neat pattern of small fields. These are the enclosed fields which, once upon a time, had been another of Helpston's former open common fields, known as Heath Field.

The Parliamentary enclosure movement which took place primarily between the middle of the eighteenth and the middle of the nineteenth centuries is a well-known aspect of English rural history. During this period several thousand parishes had their landscapes utterly transformed. Millions of acres of previously open arable fields were turned into individualised land holdings. Several more million acres of commons and wastes were also enclosed. The transformation of the land often happened very quickly, over a matter of a few short years. Surveyors arrived, got out their plans and rules, and devised a completely new arrangement to the landscape: new fields and new roads and tracks to reach them (in due course new farmhouses arrived too, set in the fields).

This process of the radical reshaping of the countryside began, as is suggested by the term Parliamentary enclosure, with an Act of Parliament. Around four thousand such 'Inclosure' Acts were passed, initially bespoke Acts for each local proposal. Much later Parliament passed a General Inclosure Act which speeded up the process and reduced the need for localised legislation.

The Parliamentary enclosure movement affected a great swathe of England, although not the whole country. Parliamentary enclosure was a feature in particular of the Midland counties, although it extended from Yorkshire in a wide belt across the heart of England down to eastern Dorset, as well as across into the western parts of East Anglia. Other parts of England, including the West Country, the Home Counties, the Welsh Marches and the lands of England's north-west and north-east had a different history in relation to enclosure, and the situation in Wales and Scotland was different again. You could say, therefore, that my journey along the Jurassic stone belt was to a large extent also a journey through the heart of the countryside most affected by Parliamentary enclosure.

Flora Thompson's Oxfordshire hamlet of Juniper Hill was one of those settlements enclosed during this period. She recalls in her book *Lark Rise* that, during her childhood in the 1880s, there were still old people in Juniper Hill who could remember the land as it had been before enclosure into arable fields: "the Rise when it stood in a wide expanse of open heath, with juniper bushes and furze thickets and close, springy, rabbit-bitten turf". This had been common land which had come under the plough for the first time after the passing of the enclosure Act, Thompson explains.

But when I had first planned my cycle route I had decided that – when it came to Parliamentary enclosure – I would wait until I was in Northamptonshire before trying to tackle the subject. There was one village, I felt, which particularly required me to make a visit. Going to Helpston did involve a slight detour from my journey north into Lincolnshire, it's true: I found myself heading eastwards to get there from Barnack and I had a strong suspicion that I was briefly leaving oolite stone territory to venture on to Jurassic limestone heathland. But Helpston's enclosure, and the effect the enclosure had on the local landscape, has become one of the best-known examples in the country. Helpston is the village where the poet John Clare was born in 1793 and where he lived until 1832, and it is in some of Clare's poems that we get a powerful sense of the effect that enclosure could bring about.

The Inclosure Act of 1809 which covered Helpston (and some adjoining parishes) was passed when Clare was in his teens. The new road system was staked out in 1811, the field allotment process made a year later and the minor roads begun a year after that. Enclosure in Helpston was effectively completed by 1820, the year when Clare's first book of poetry was published and when he began to receive acclaim for his work. By this stage Clare was in his late twenties.

In other words, the traditional landscape which Helpston had known for many centuries was transformed during a particularly formative time in Clare's life. Clare was a self-taught poet whose background was in the local agricultural community. He knew the Helpston landscape intimately and he had a keen understanding of the natural world. His father was a casual farm labourer and Clare himself worked in the fields when he was a teenager. His memorial described him as the 'Northamptonshire Peasant Poet', a term which raises questions of exactly what we might mean by an English peasantry but certainly is far more appropriately attributed to Clare than, say, to William Barnes in Dorset. (There's something else about Clare's memorial citation which can raise an issue: Helpston since Clare's day has been moved out of Northamptonshire to become, firstly, part of an enlarged Cambridgeshire and now administratively part of the Peterborough unitary authority. Despite this, Northamptonshire still likes to claim Clare as its own.)

Clare's first two books of poems were widely reviewed and very successful, and he was taken up and patronised by London literary circles, perhaps on the basis that he could become an English equivalent of Robert Burns. Later, as it often does, literary fashion moved on and Clare stopped being lionised – ironically, given that his poetry was getting better at this point. As most people today who know of Clare are aware, his later life included periods of mental ill-health that saw him confined to asylums, firstly in Epping Forest and then in Northampton. His was certainly a troubled life. He died in 1864. He is still remembered in his native village, however. The cottage where he was born in Helpston has been acquired in recent years by a local charity, the John Clare Trust, and is now a small visitor centre dedicated to his memory.

Clare wrote a number of early poems which describe the transformation of Helpston at the time when the enclosure process was still in full swing.

However the poems which arguably tackle the theme of enclosure most successfully were written later, in mid-life. One of his most striking turns of phrase comes in the poem *Remembrances*:

> Inclosure like a buonaparte let not a thing remain
> It levelled every bush and tree and levelled every hill
> And hung the moles for traitors – though the brook is running still
> It runs a naked stream cold and chill.

Remembrances was one of a series of poems he wrote in the mid-1830s as he made the move for the first time away from Helpston village. Another, often considered one of his very best poems, was called *The Mores* [the Moors]. Clare begins this poem by celebrating the wide open expanses which he had known before the process of enclosure (following Clare, I will leave his verse unpunctuated and the spelling unchanged):

> Far spread the moorey ground a level scene
> Bespread with rush and one eternal green
> That never felt the rage of blundering plough
> Though centurys wreathed springs blossoms on its brow
> Still meeting plains that stretched them far away
> In uncheckt shadows of green brown and grey

The landscape, Clare goes on, was one that was unfettered and unencumbered in stark contrast to the scene after enclosure:

> Unbounded freedom ruled the wandering scene
> Nor fence of ownership crept in between
> To hide the prospect of the following eye
> Its only bondage was the circling sky

These unenclosed common fields stretched out, away to the distant horizon:

> One mighty flat undwarfed by bush and tree
> Spread its faint shadow of immensity
> And lost itself which seemed to eke its bounds
> In the blue mist the orisons edge surrounds.

But the landscape which Clare knew from his childhood and which he celebrates here had changed:

Now this sweet vision of my boyish hours
Free as spring clouds and wild as summer flowers
Is faded all – a hope that blossomed free
And hath been once no more shall ever be
Inclosure came and trampled on the grave
Of labours rights and left the poor a slave...

These are powerfully felt and powerfully expressed emotions, and though to an extent there is an element of longing for a lost childhood in these poems to which the pre-enclosure landscape becomes a convenient backdrop, Clare was clear on his assessment that enclosure had been a process led by greed. As Clare put it in another poem, "Inclosure thou'rt a curse upon the land".

A curse? Parliamentary enclosure was very controversial at the time it was taking place (indeed, the reason Parliamentary legislation was necessary was because in most villages those promoting enclosure were up against others with local land rights or commoners' rights who vehemently opposed the change). Enclosure has also been a contentious area of history for subsequent historians. For many years the dominant view among social historians, expressed initially by Barbara and John Hammond in their influential 1911 book *The Village Labourer,* was that enclosure had worked to the benefit of the rich landowners, impoverishing those with only small land rights and completely dispossessing those who had previously enjoyed grazing and other commoners' rights on the common lands. These often long-established rights of custom, because they were not legally documented, were generally disregarded when land was reallocated after enclosure.

Enclosure, the argument has gone, led to the development of a downtrodden workforce of agricultural labourers in rural areas who lost their independence and became dependent on employment by others for their livelihood. Indirectly, through encouraging migration off the land, enclosure also led to the growth of the industrial working class in urban areas.

This assessment of the results of enclosure has been picked over and sometimes criticised by later historians and to some extent the arguments in academic quarters rumble on. Some would claim that, whatever the social costs, enclosure helped make English agriculture more productive. Sheer self-preservation means that I hesitate to barge in to this particular debate. Fortunately I can lean instead on the work of the historian Jeanette Neeson who, more than anyone else, has subjected the enclosures which took place in the county of Northamptonshire – including the enclosure in Helpston – to detailed scrutiny. Her 1993 book *Commoners* reviewed the evidence and came to a very firm conclusion: "In most of the villages studied here parliamentary enclosure destroyed the old peasant economy. It did this not only by more than decimating small occupiers and landlords and by reducing their total acreage, but also by more completely separating the agricultural practice of small and large farmers, by pushing the smaller occupiers into the market more thoroughly than before, and by expropriating landless commoners on whom much of the old economy had depended...Enclosure, sanctioned by law, propagandized by the Board of Agriculture, and profited in by Members of Parliament, was the final blow to peasants in common-field England."

Perhaps we should at this point turn from social history back to the landscape. The first point to make perhaps is that, just as enclosure had its proponents and opponents, not everyone felt the same way as John Clare about what was being done to the appearance of the land. Some contemporary observers actually thought that the landscape had benefited from enclosure. There was a neatness, a tidiness now to the land which suggested human endeavour and efficiency. Where was the attraction in large common fields, what one Northamptonshire clergyman described as 'unbroken tracts [that] strained and tortured the sight'?

The writer and propagandist William Cobbett whom we last met up with in Frome couldn't quite make up his mind. Sometimes enclosure is at a receiving end of a proper Cobbett lashing: here he is near Horsham in 1823, for example, raging at the way a large common has been "cut up, disfigured, spoiled, and the labourers all driven from its skirts". On the other hand a year earlier he had been riding through Hertfordshire and reported: "Immediately upon quitting Royston, you come along, for a considerable distance, with enclosed fields on the left and open common-fields on the right. Here the land is excellent... The fields on the left seem to have been enclosed by act of parliament; and they certainly are the most beautiful tract of fields that I ever saw. Their extent may be from ten to thirty acres each. Divided by quick-set hedges, exceedingly well planted and raised... The cultivation neat..."

Today this enclosed landscape is so familiar to us that it can seem an utterly natural feature of the English countryside rather than what it really is, something created by humans two centuries or so ago. Indeed, I think Middle England would rise up in utter horror if it was to be proposed today, let's say, to destroy the field systems, grub up the hedges and restore the original common-field system of pre-enclosure Britain. I'm conscious of how even relatively modest plans to change the landscape – as for example we saw at East Coker for the proposed new housing south of Yeovil – bring forth vehement protest.

Looking back from today's perspective, therefore, it seems extraordinary at just how radical a change to a large part of England and its landscape could successfully be pushed through, albeit against protests and objections. At the time of Parliamentary enclosure, the country's politicians and those who elected them seemed prepared to sacrifice the past in the name of progress; by contrast, today the default position seems to be one of preservation and heritage.

Sleaford

I had a late lunch that day in Stamford, in a café down near the river which provided me with an over-priced sandwich served up with potato crisps and tired salad on a wooden platter. It took an age to come.

I was in a hurry. This was the penultimate day of my journey and it was the one where I'd planned to cram in the most mileage. I'd started out from Kettering, and with the extra miles to Barnack and Helpston and back I reckoned that I had already done over fifty miles. My evening accommodation was booked at a B&B in Sleaford, more than thirty miles further into Lincolnshire. It was time to press on.

I left Stamford travelling almost due north, picking up the quiet B1176 a few miles out of the town. For a time I cycled alongside the East Coast main line, the railway which the Earl of Exeter had managed to exclude from Stamford itself. Small villages came and went; Careby, Little Bytham, Swinstead, Irnham, Ingoldsby.

I'd come prepared for those technical problems which can affect cyclists and which they refer to in the Tour de France as mechanicals. Ever since Burton Bradstock I had carried a spare inner tube and a set of tyre levers to cope with punctures. I had a few other tools which I hoped might serve in an emergency. Perhaps more important, I'd drawn up beforehand a list of all the cycle shops along my route.

But my bike behaved itself immaculately. From Dorset to the Humber no tyres became flat, no brake cables snapped. No bits fell off. And by this stage in the trip I felt in good condition too. The weather had been kind to me and day by day I'd upped the mileage, feeling strong. It helped perhaps that the hills were left behind: Lincolnshire (whatever they may tell you) is not a flat county but on the other hand it doesn't have gradients of 25% or worse to throw at its cyclists. Powerstock and the Dorset hills were a long way astern.

On the other hand, every cyclist knows to be prepared for the unexpected.

Somewhere in the quiet by-road I was following, as I cycled along enjoying the sensation of the wind on my face, I felt a rather different sensation: I realised after a moment that I had been stung on my upper lip. It was, I assume, a bee which had found itself unable to escape my onrush (it must have been because of the astonishingly fast speed at which I was undoubtedly propelling my bicycle). For the next twenty-four hours my lip swelled up impressively. I fear though that the bee came out of the encounter the worst.

With some relief sometime in the late afternoon I found myself on the approach into Sleaford and a few minutes later was being welcomed at the B&B. The bike had been safely stored in a shed in the back garden and my panniers were once again being unpacked, the contents strewn over the bed. The end of the last-day-but-one. Just one more day's cycling to go.

It was my first visit to Sleaford, a pleasant market town with, I gathered, a history which goes back to prehistoric times. Sleaford is the perhaps unlikely location for the National Centre for Craft and Design, a strikingly interesting modern building tagged on to an old seed warehouse. I managed to squeeze in a quick visit before it closed for the day. I liked the place. There were several large exhibition galleries that I enjoyed wandering through as well as a craft shop selling high-quality contemporary works and, of course, a café. Almost without exception the staff were young and extremely fashionably dressed. This felt like metropolitan London: momentarily I felt that I had left Middle England behind.

I returned through the quiet Sleaford streets feeling that somebody had done a very good job in finding the grant funding to bring the National Centre to this corner of Lincolnshire. I hope it's appreciated locally. I hope it's sustainable.

The warehouse which has now found a new role for itself in this way is the most impressive building in what was once the wharf in the centre of the town. Sleaford had its own waterway, the Sleaford Navigation, a canalised version of the original river Slea which ran for twelve miles roughly eastwards until it met the navigable river Witham. It was opened in 1794 and was officially abandoned in 1878, although parts remained usable into the twentieth century. But in Sleaford, as in other parts of the country, there's a strong community push behind the idea of reopening the navigation once again. Campaigning started in the early 1970s and a society, the Sleaford Navigation Trust, was set up a few years later. There have been successes: much of the eastern end of the navigation has now been reopened to boats and work has been done at the Sleaford end to bring water back into what had become little more than overgrown ditches. There is still a gap in the middle awaiting renovation, although the Trust says that kayakers can make it all the way through. There is a potential tourist prize to be won if and when the work is fully completed: Sleaford would then be once again connected to Lincoln and Boston by navigable waterway – which means that it too could be part of that prospective Fens Waterways Link.

The Navigation is work in progress. But some in the community in Sleaford are also doing what they can to promote an existing important transport link, the railway.

Sleaford doesn't do badly in terms of its rail links: the town is on the Nottingham-Skegness branch line, which often can be a sleepy affair but sometimes (summer weekends and bank holidays) can see trains packed out with holidaymakers wanting to get to that bracing sea air on the Lincolnshire coast. There's another railway line from the town going north and offering services to Lincoln and Newark. Finally there's a railway which goes off to the south (if only for limited periods each day) to Spalding and Peterborough. Some people would like a much more frequent through service up from Peterborough to Doncaster via Sleaford, offering a sort of alternative to the main East Coast line a little way away to the west.

As in other rural parts of the country, there's a sense that railway lines in country areas like Lincolnshire need a little TLC, and the Nottingham-Sleaford-Skegness line has its own Community Rail Partnership trying to provide just that. This is an idea which began more than twenty years ago and which has now been adopted right across Britain, from the line to St Ives in Cornwall to the Friends of the Far North Line helping keep the railway serving Thurso and Wick.

The Community Rail Partnership for the line through Sleaford to Skegness was set up in 2005 and over the years since then has tried out various ideas to get more local engagement with the line. Perhaps the highest profile activity is the now-regular Music Train, held normally each month on a Thursday evening when one or more musicians board the train at Sleaford and perform during the fifty minute journey to the small station of Wainfleet. That station is very conveniently only a short walk away from Batemans brewery, which equally conveniently has its own brewery tap which is opened for the occasion. A return train leaves Wainfleet more than an hour later to get passengers, by now presumably somewhat sozzled, safely home. I was told that a similar idea had been tried for a speed-dating Love Train some years back, although I got the distinct impression it hadn't been quite so successful – perhaps not everyone who is single in the east Midlands is quite so keen on railways or real ale. Not every idea to promote rural railways necessarily works.

Community input to the railways makes obvious sense, Peter Roberts told me when I met him in a café in one of Sleaford's main streets. Peter is the current Chairman of the national network of community rail organisations, the Association of Community Rail Partnerships (ACoRP), and as he also lives in Sleaford this seemed like an interview I should bag while I had the chance: an opportunity to find out what was happening not just in this part of Lincolnshire but also further afield.

We began with a little history. Community engagement in railway partnerships (and the related concept of Friends groups established to look after particular local stations) began in the 1990s at a time when there was dark talk of a second wave of Beeching-style axing of branch lines. That risk was averted, and indeed Peter told me that the concept of getting communities involved in supporting their local lines has been so successful that it is now a formal part of the government's approach to the railways. The recently adopted governmental Community Rail Development Strategy not only acknowledges the role which community engagement plays but even imposes an obligation on rail franchise holders to put resources into railway partnerships and Friends schemes in their franchise areas.

There are now around 50 community rail partnerships together covering more than eighty lines, and there are also 1000 or so Friends of Stations groups. Peter claimed that community rail partnerships more than pay for themselves in terms of both economic and social value, showing me the results of research ACoRP had undertaken a few years back. Did I know, he asked me, that there are 3,200 community volunteers around the country giving 250,000 hours of voluntary time a year in support? Stations are being redeveloped and becoming vibrant centres of community life. I nodded. I was prepared to accept without too much persuading that this was a good idea.

If you're thinking of setting up a community rail partnership it helps, I quickly realised, to have a strong marketing name for what you're doing. Peter had presented me with a map of all the groups who participate in the ACoRP network, so I noted that the Avocet Line is the name given to the line from Exeter to Exmouth. The Bittern Line turns out to be the railway from Norwich to Sheringham. And the Rail Partnership through Sleaford to Skegness? This has been formally named as the Poacher Line.

Because of course: we are in the land of the *Lincolnshire Poacher*, one of those folk songs which most people (if they don't actually know the words) feel that they at least *ought* to know them. Let me remind you how it starts:

When I was bound apprentice in famous Lincolnshire
Full well I served my master, for more than seven year
Till I took up to poaching, as you shall quickly hear
Oh, 'tis my delight on a shining night, in the season of the year.

The *Lincolnshire Poacher* was a popular song of the time which, because songs like these tended to be printed originally on large sheets of paper, we now usually describe as broadsheet ballads. (The song of the agricultural trade unionists in Somerset I mentioned many chapters back comes from the same tradition, although the *Lincolnshire Poacher* predates it by at least a century: the earliest printed version of the song that's been found dates from the 1770s.)

There are a lot of songs about poaching which came out as broadsheet ballads, and generally they are full of the woes of transportation which await those who are caught. The *Lincolnshire Poacher* is somewhat unusual in being cheerfully upbeat (this particular episode of poaching ends not with the miscreant hauled up before unfeeling magistrates, but with a hare being caught and sold quietly to a neighbour in exchange for five shillings). That, and the enjoyably catchy tune, is perhaps why the song has had a very respectable after-life, being used today among other things as a regimental marching tune. Poachers, you feel, are now a century or more beyond being threatening to anyone. They can safely enter the realms of entertaining folk heroes: cheeky chaps, rather in the mode of Robin Hood.

In reality, poaching was a significant part of rural life for the eighteenth and nineteenth centuries and undertaking it was a pretty desperate business. A caught rabbit, or better, could provide meat on the table for agricultural workers who normally had to survive on much more paltry fare. On the other hand a caught *poacher* would face the potential prospect of banishment through transportation to a convict colony in Van Diemen's Land (Tasmania) or the like – or, for the unlucky, of being sentenced to death and hanged.

Legal historians look back today at the acts of parliament which were passed to protect game during this period and shake their heads in disbelief at the draconic nature of the penalties. It was the Whig government under

Walpole who in May 1723 brought in a law, technically known as 9 George I c.22 but more often known as the Black Act, which mopped up in its clauses a whole range of provisions for poaching and which introduced the death penalty for many such offences. It was so loosely drafted that, as time went by, more and more activities could send you to the gallows. It passed through Parliament in a matter of weeks.

The Black Act was eventually repealed, but the Night Poaching Act of 1828 is still in force today. In fact, there was big excitement in the national media in 2007 at the time of the trial of two men in Herefordshire who had been caught by police in the early hours of a morning with nineteen rabbits in their possession. Under the 1828 Act, the press reported, the men could have been "transported beyond seas for seven years or be kept in hard labour in the common gaols for two years" had they failed to pay the fine. Sensibly, they chose to apologise to the court and paid up.

I can't now recall whether it was a shining night or not the evening I was in Sleaford, but I wasn't tempted to try my own hand at a little Lincolnshire poaching. I was too tired from the day's efforts. I slept soundly in my B&B, and woke ready for the final day's journey. From Sleaford through Lincoln to the Humber: that was what I had ahead.

Branston

You probably don't need me to tell you that agriculture is important in Lincolnshire. The county produces an eighth of the country's food and has proportionately more top quality agricultural land than anywhere else. So it's time perhaps to say something more about farming and the effect it inevitably has on the way this part of England looks and feels.

When I was in Bathampton, you'll recall, I visited the Dry Arch community cooperative with their six acres of land. You couldn't get further from the Dry Arch growers than some of the massive agricultural holdings in Lincolnshire. The county has well over a thousand farms with more than a hundred hectares of land (roughly 250 acres), the largest category of farm that government statistics record. The trend in recent years has been towards increasing field sizes and increasing farm sizes. This has helped generate increased food production, but as Lincolnshire county council points out it's also had other consequences. Hedgerows and wetlands have disappeared and the high levels of use of fertilisers and weed and pest control chemicals have in some areas led to pollution of ground water supplies. What goes on here would certainly not meet Colin Tudge's definition of 'real farming': agri-business in Lincolnshire does, however, provide food *en masse* which supermarkets can sell at very low prices. At the moment this seems to be what most of us care most about.

My route from Sleaford northwards took me on a series of minor roads through rich agricultural farmland. A few miles before I reached Lincoln, however, the fields gave way to a large development of offices and industrial units. It was a working day, and the place was receiving deliveries from a steady flow of HGVs (when you are cycling, you notice HGVs). I was intrigued. As I cycled past I noticed that the company took its name from the nearby village of Branston, and I decided when I had a chance to find out more. What precisely went on in this industrial corner of rural Lincolnshire?

The answer, I discovered, is potatoes. If you buy bags of spuds in Tesco, there's a very good chance that the vegetables will have been sorted and packed in the industrial buildings I had passed at Branston. The company ("if it's to do with potatoes, we do it," says their website) has the responsibility of supplying roughly three-quarters of Tesco's potato stocks. Waitrose buys from Branston, too, as does the Booker wholesale chain and some of the Co-operative stores. The company with its six hundred staff turns over £100m a year, pretty well entirely on the basis of the British love of potatoes.

Later on Branston kindly offered to show me round their plant. I was equipped with the usual safety clothing and boots, and – feeling a little like a politician doing one of those factory visits for the benefit of the TV cameras – was taken into the working end of the building. I saw where the potatoes arrive from the growers, packed into large wooden boxes and brought by the lorries I had avoided when I was cycling. I saw the warming shed where the potatoes are kept at between ten and twelve degrees, in the dark to avoid growth. I saw the machine which gently shakes off the excess soil and removes any stones that have come too. I was shown the washing equipment, the conveyor belts that move the potatoes through to the grading machines, and then the so-called singulation process where each remaining individual potato is carried forward towards the weighing machines. Of course it's all a heavily automated process but there are also staff working here, checking the quality of the vegetables as they travel past on the belts and if necessary removing any rotten potatoes which have slipped through (the duff spuds get taken off to an anaerobic digester plant on site, which provides all the energy used by the company).

Eventually the potatoes reach the weighing and packing area. Here I could see 1.75kg bags of King Edwards coming off the machines, ready branded with Tesco's name and all set to be trucked down to the supermarket's Dagenham depot. Within days they'd be in the shops.

Potatoes are, of course, our traditional staple diet in Britain. We buy them in supermarkets and greengrocers to cook at home, we buy them packeted up in the frozen food section of supermarkets, we buy them in crisp packets, we buy them when we go to fish and chip shops or other fast food places, and we buy them increasingly in pre-prepared food, in all the shepherd's pies and fish pies which we stick in our microwaves when we can't think what else to eat. But we actually buy fewer potatoes than we once did. Pasta, and rice, and fashions for things like low-carb diets have taken their toll. Purchases of potatoes are down 18% on what they were ten years ago, and there has been a 10% decline in just the last five years.

Once upon a time there was the Potato Marketing Board. That was abolished some years ago and now the industry is overseen by a section of the Agriculture and Horticulture Development Board, which helpfully provides all the facts you could ever want to know about potatoes and the British. It was AHDB data which confirmed the on-going shift towards large-scale growing. Currently over half of the potato crop comes from farmers who have 100 hectares or more of fields growing potatoes, about double the position twenty years ago. At the same time – as you'd predict – the total number of growers is falling.

Perhaps significantly, the variety of potato being grown is falling too. Not so long ago you would have had the choice of around thirty types of potatoes when you went to the shops; today Britain focuses on around fifteen varieties, with Maris Piper far and away the most popular. Does this matter? Isn't a potato fundamentally just a potato? Perhaps it is. Is it just sentimentality to suggest that we might yet come to regret the loss?

As consumers we pay (thank you once again, AHDB) an average of 83p for a kilogramme of fresh potatoes, £1.36 a kg for frozen chips and over £6.63 a kg for potatoes which have been converted into crisps. What does the grower get? The answer, I discovered when I met with Branston's managing director James Truscott, is that it all depends. If you're unlucky and have to sell on the open market when prices are depressed you might get £100 a tonne (10p a kg) or even less; if you sell when prices are inflated, you could get £400 a tonne. This is what's called the free-buy market which operates entirely on the basis of supply and demand and is very influenced by factors such as the time of year and the weather. But James Truscott told me that much of the potato crop is already pre-sold under contract at an agreed price. Some of his 140 suppliers, he told me, arrange to sell all their crop to Branston in this way, at the price Branston fixes before the season starts. Others may sell 50% under contract and then take a chance on the open market price. 2015 and 2016 saw relatively high prices; on the other hand, 2014 and 2013 saw prices very low. If you're a grower you also need to take account of storage costs; most potatoes are released on the market only after they have been lifted and stored, sometimes for months. Some farmers have their own storage sheds, others use the services of packaging companies such as Branston. Either way there is a cost involved.

Branston was originally founded, James Truscott told me, as a farmers' co-operative before converting into a private company with some of the original farmers now as shareholders. James Truscott himself went into the food industry after university and before joining Branston in 2013 worked for major companies such as Unilever and Kerry Foods and for a time for Tesco's Californian subsidiary. He's worried that agriculture and food processing isn't seen by today's young people as a good place to build a career and his firm works with the local secondary school in the village of Branston to try to remedy this, giving sixth formers there an idea of what the company does. We need software experts for our business systems team, he tells me. We employ an agronomy team who go out to work with farmers on improving their crops, he adds. It's not just the low-paid work on the conveyor belts or the packing rooms.

But on the other hand Branston, like almost all the major agri-business companies in Lincolnshire, does have its fair share of jobs like these, and – again like other local firms – finds it hard to recruit enough local people to do this work. Fortunately for the firm, there's been the option in recent years of using migrant labour from elsewhere in the European Union. Branston is not as dependent on migrant workers as some agricultural companies (horticulture growers especially are particularly reliant on help at crop-picking time) but nevertheless around 40% of its staff are from other EU countries. They are excellent members of the team, James says, who have been building their careers with us.

So what's going to happen now, following the 2016 referendum? James Truscott would potentially face the same dilemma as Julian Palmer at the Tinker's Barn quarry at Naunton were EU workers suddenly to be removed from the workforce, and he admits that his overseas staff have been worried at the implications. The reality seems to be, though, that the agri-food business is so dependent on migrant labour that the government will have to come up with some workable fix. Before 2014 the country had a Seasonal Agricultural Workers Scheme, primarily to help out the horticulture sector. Something similar, it seems, may have to be brought back. But firms such as Branston are also affected by the government's recent increases in the minimum hourly wage rate, the so-called living wage. In the medium term, James Truscott predicts, the low paid jobs will disappear. Stand by for the arrival of robotics in agriculture.

A recent news story in the local press about job creation by Branston brought in a sour comment online from a reader who asked how many of the new jobs would be there for local British people. Anti-migrant feeling is a reality in Lincolnshire (perhaps not helped by high levels of media attention; the Daily Mail in 2013 ran a story on Boston which carried the provocative headline "The town that's had enough" and which quoted one local woman who claimed that she now lived in a 'foreign country').

There's clearly an issue here to be addressed. Local people need to feel they are being listened to. The migrant workers who are so essential for the Lincolnshire agricultural and horticultural economy need to be listened to as well, and measures put in place to ensure they are not subject to exploitative treatment. Sadly, the tensions which can be perceived today in Lincolnshire are not necessarily new ones. I found an account of the experiences of early seventeenth-century groups of Protestant refugees from northern France and the Spanish-controlled Low Countries who settled in the fenlands in northern Lincolnshire, where they undertook work in reclaiming land from the fens, creating agricultural land and building houses. They weren't welcomed. In 1642, according to one contemporary report, local people destroyed the houses and opened the flood gates to let the water back into the land, threatening to "stay till the whole level was drowned and the inhabitants were forced to swim away like ducks". Oh dear. English landscape history is not always the happy tale one would wish to recount.

Lincoln

I was looking at a large slab of Inferior Oolite limestone which had recently been cut from a small quarry just to the north of Lincoln city centre and which, a hundred and seventy million years or so after it had first been formed, was about to begin a new life as a voussoir.

A voussoir, if like me your architectural vocabulary is not all that it might be, is a wedge-shaped stone used in the construction of an arch. This particular voussoir was destined to have a modest role to play in Lincoln's most impressive building, its cathedral.

Lincoln cathedral is unique among British cathedrals in having its own quarry, there to provide the local stone needed for the endless work of restoration. Indeed in the years since the 1980s, when the cathedral authorities first began taking the stone, so much has been removed that the quarry is now almost exhausted and the cathedral's head mason Paul Booth has been scouring the local area for a replacement. It's not easy: there is plenty of stone still under the ground in what's called uphill Lincoln but unfortunately getting to it would mean demolishing the often historic houses on the top. Paul Booth has had to look to the south of the city instead. The advice of geologists and geophysicists has been sought and a potential site, at present used for agriculture, has been identified. Landowners have been talked to. The trial drilling is about to begin. Lincoln cathedral looks set to continue to have the stone it needs to maintain the building for many years to come.

This must be a good thing, because when it comes to long-term strategic planning Lincoln cathedral can teach the rest of us a thing or two. When I meet Paul Booth in the masons' workshop just on the edge of the cathedral close he tells me that there is what amounts to a hundred-year plan in place for restoration and conservation work. He has, he adds, just finished work on the projections for major work on the cathedral's three towers: the work is scheduled to begin in 2037 and to last for twelve years.

Lincoln cathedral dominates its city in a way which, I think, no other English cathedral can claim to do. You might, I suppose, conceivably argue the case for Durham, or Salisbury, or even Ely Cathedral when viewed from the flat lands surrounding the town, but nevertheless there is something extraordinarily powerful about the siting of Lincoln's cathedral on the steep little hill at the north end of the city. A pamphlet I picked up inside at the cathedral bookshop gives John Ruskin's opinion: "I have always held and am prepared against all evidence to maintain that the Cathedral of Lincoln is out and out the most precious piece of architecture in the British Isles and roughly speaking worth any two other cathedrals we have".

The cathedral was first constructed a few years after the Norman Conquest, being consecrated in 1092. Of course, there has been plenty of history since then: a fire in 1141 which led to rebuilding work, an earthquake in 1185 which destroyed much of the edifice and led to more rebuilding, the collapse of the original central tower around 1237, a storm in 1548 which took off the spire which had originally topped this rebuilt tower, and so on. Two smaller spires on the west towers were taken down early in the nineteenth century as a precaution, considered too costly to repair. Nevertheless what we see today is more or less the same as what Lincoln people have been looking at for the past four centuries or more.

If we start examining the cathedral in close-up, however, when we get down to the level of the stones themselves, we find a constant process of renewal going on. The north-west Turret, for example, has just had the scaffolding removed after work to clean and replace some of the stones there. New carvings, on the suitably Lincolnshire theme of food and farming, have been put in place, carved by some of Paul Booth's team of fourteen stonemasons. Now his attention is moving to the flying buttress on the north-west transept, where conservation work carried out by the Victorians is itself beginning to fail.

I find coping with the maintenance responsibilities of looking after my own home hard enough, so I am impressed that there are people who can take on the task of ensuring that a building which is more than eighty metres high doesn't tumble down around the heads of the Dean and the Chapter at prayer. Paul Booth says that he and the cathedral's architect separately inspect the building on a stone-by-stone basis, and then compare notes. They are looking for failing stones, those which have to be dealt with. Out of respect for earlier generations of masons, everything else will be left in place.

But are there really any parts of the cathedral where the original mediaeval stone is still there, I ask Paul? He says that there probably are, tucked away in parts of the building which are sheltered from the weather, adding that the original cathedral included Purbeck stone, from further along the Jurassic coast in Dorset. Repair work over the centuries has used a variety of different stone, including some stone which was brought in from France in the twentieth century before the cathedral acquired its own quarry. But you sense that Paul Booth is pleased that the work he is overseeing is able to use stone from Lincoln itself.

Not that the Inferior Oolite stone is easy to work, he tells me. Like many masons he moved for his career when he was younger, gaining experience around the world before returning to Britain. He has worked with sandstone, with Chinese stone and with Cumbrian slate and red sandstone, he says, and when he first came to Lincoln to become head mason a few years back (still only in his late thirties) it took him time to get a feel for the local oolite. "You have to learn the stone. It's the feel of it. With every blow from the mallet and chisel you have to change, to get the contours of the stone and to learn its density. If I give the stone to an apprentice, it will take them a week to get used to it," he says. "But once you get used to it, it's so rewarding," he adds.

Being a stonemason, he explains to me, isn't the same as being a sculptor. There may be scope for a little ornamentation, perhaps, when stones are being carved, but much of the work is about geometry, carving the stone to the detailed plans which have been drawn up in the office where the draughtsmanship takes place. First come the plans, I gathered. Then the plans go to the quarry, so that the appropriate stone can be identified and cut to size. Then the banker masons carve the stone, in the cathedral workshop. Finally the fixer masons take the new stones to the building itself, to be put in place. Paul Booth has the oversight of this process: "It's a wonderful responsibility – I bless it every day," he says.

The stonemasons at Lincoln are unusual in being directly employed by the cathedral (increasingly English cathedrals are looking to outsource this work to independent specialist companies). This makes Paul Booth and his colleagues part of a significant cathedral workforce of around 150, with a concomitant wage bill. Cathedrals are curious institutions, effectively independent of the usual structures of the Church of England and self-governing under a complex structure made up (since 1999) of the Chapter, the Council and a College of Canons. The Dean is the boss on the spiritual side of things, but Lincoln cathedral also has a chief executive to run the business – except that the current holder of the office prefers to call herself the Chapter Clerk. Other cathedrals have had high-profile financial difficulties recently and indeed in 2017 the Church of England set up a working group to explore whether cathedrals need to change the way they are governed. Lincoln, it seems, manages at the moment to be self-financing. Unusually it charges tourists to enter the cathedral, and it has other fund-raising ideas to tease more money out of visitors. You can, for example, 'adopt a stone' for a gift of £25 or more; occasionally, for a donation of £2000 or more, you can also directly sponsor a new carving. I am sure Paul Booth and his team will make a good job of it.

Gainsthorpe

From Lincoln to journey's end at Winteringham involved another forty miles or so of cycling. I could probably have saved a few miles had I taken the direct route which runs straight from Lincoln north all the way, and which for much of the way is the A15. 'Straight' is the word, for the modern road follows the line of the Roman road Ermine Street. But it's a busy road. I read somewhere that Lincolnshire sees 360,000 journeys by HGVs full of agricultural produce through the county each year, and I was keen to mingle with as few of those HGVs as possible.

Instead I took another ancient route north from Lincoln, a by-road which almost certainly dates back into prehistoric times, long before the Romans came and engineered Ermine Street. The B1398 is a delightful back road that runs along the western edge of an escarpment known locally as The Cliff. Any idea you may have that Lincolnshire is dead flat is rapidly corrected if you come this way: the ground drops quite sharply off the ridge to the fields which in places are more than forty metres below.

The Cliff is an escarpment which runs more or less directly south-north from Lincoln and which, if you look on the British Geological Survey online map, is represented by a corridor of colour right up to Winteringham on the Humber: pale yellow to represent Inferior Oolite. This higher ground made an obvious route north in prehistoric times, and indeed the Jurassic Way is the collective name given to the network of tracks which were used in Early Bronze Age time and which may have begun to be walked for the first time in the Neolithic period. My B-road was following one of these tracks, a route which has its own name of Middle Street.

I enjoyed Middle Street. I enjoyed the views down to my west, and I took pleasure as each little village came and went: Scampton, Aisthorpe, Brattleby, Cammeringham. Eventually I reached the tiny market town of Kirton Lindsey where I stopped for a sandwich in the local baker's shop.

Nothing much appears to happen in Kirton Lindsey, although it does boast a railway station a little out of the town centre – with a total of five trains every week, and then only on Saturdays. Three trains head west and two trains east.

For almost all my cycle ride from Dorset the weather had been perfect: pleasant dry days, not too hot but certainly not too cold. This was weather which required nothing more than a short-sleeved cycling top and shorts. But somewhere along Middle Street the drizzle began, and by Kirton Lindsey the rain was beginning to set in. When I stopped at Gainsthorpe, a few miles further north, I had already put on arm-warmers and a waterproof. Gainsthorpe greeted me with a cold wind and low clouds, but perhaps in the circumstances this was the appropriate weather for the place.

There is, in fact, little to see at Gainsthorpe, but that is rather the point. Gainsthorpe is a deserted mediaeval village, the lumps and humps of earthworks which represent what were once cottages and yards ('tofts') and enclosed paddocks ('crofts') now safely looked after by English Heritage. Gainsthorpe was being lived in at the time of the Domesday Book in 1086 and by 1208 had acquired a chapel and a windmill. There appears to have been a farm, perhaps a manorial farm, with a fishpond and two dovecotes. But the last time the village is recorded in mediaeval times was in 1383. At some point something happened to the people and the place. Gainsthorpe died.

It's not clear why Gainsthorpe became deserted, but there are various possibilities. Some mediaeval villages were never repopulated after the ravages of the plague. The worst epidemic was the Black Death which arrived in Britain from mainland Europe in 1348 and between then and 1350 killed an estimated 1.5 million people (the total population was only around four million). The plague returned thereafter in 1361-62 and at other times in the fourteenth and fifteenth centuries with the last major outbreak being the Great Plague of London in 1665. The people of Gainsthorpe may have been struck down by one of these epidemics.

It's also possible that Gainsthorpe was depopulated because of soil erosion, effectively because the land no longer became economically able to sustain its population. There is a third possibility, however: that Gainsthorpe was deliberately depopulated by its landowner who turfed out the villagers in order to convert the land to the more profitable business of sheep grazing. This certainly was what happened to other villages in mediaeval times, including some nearby.

I described the Parliamentary enclosure movement when I was in Helpston, aided by the poetry of John Clare. But enclosure was a process which, in many parts of England, had long predated the Parliamentary enclosure period. Much of the south-east of England, including Kent, Essex and parts of Surrey and Suffolk, were enclosed by the sixteenth century, as was most of the south-west, the English counties abutting the Welsh border and Lancashire and parts of North Yorkshire too. Indeed enclosure had been going on since at least the thirteenth century, the process accelerating in the fifteenth and sixteenth centuries. In many cases the economic driver behind enclosure was the desire to create pasture for sheep.

The most famous critique of enclosure in the pre-Parliamentary enclosure period comes in Thomas More's book *Utopia*, originally written in Latin and published in 1516 (it was translated into English in 1551). More's book depicts a fictional island society, but his purpose (as with all later writers who try to depict utopian societies) is also to point a finger of satire or criticism at aspects of his own society. Here is More, in the guise of the narrator, recounting a particularly English form of 'stealing':

'Forsooth, my lord' (quoth I), 'your sheep that were wont to be so meek and tame, and so small eaters, now, as I hear say, be become so great devourers and so wild that they eat up and swallow down the very men themselves. They consume, destroy, and devour whole fields, houses, and cities. For look in what parts of the realm doth grow the finest, and therefore dearest wool, there noblemen and gentlemen, yea, and certain abbots, holy men, no doubt, not contenting themselves with the yearly revenues and profits that were wont to grow to their forefathers and predecessors of their lands, nor being content that they live in rest and pleasure nothing profiting, yea much annoying the weal public, leave no ground for tillage, they enclose all into pastures; they throw down houses; they pluck down towns, and leave nothing standing, but only the church to be made a sheephouse...'

More goes on to depict the sorry tale of the villagers forced to leave their homes: "wretched souls, men, women, husbands, wives, fatherless children, widows, woeful mothers with their young babes, and their whole household... away they trudge, I say, out of their known and accustomed houses, finding no place to rest in".

Just occasionally, at different times during this period of enclosure, villagers at the receiving end of the treatment didn't just trudge away in silence. It can be argued that resistance to enclosure was a factor, if not the primary motive, behind the Peasants' Revolt of 1381 but certainly by the time of the uprising in Norfolk in 1549 led by yeoman farmer Robert Kett enclosure had become the central issue. Kett's rebellion, as it is usually referred to, began with a group of protesters destroying fences which had been put up by local landowners, and grew in numbers until perhaps 16,000 people were involved. Kett and his informal army of rebels captured the city of Norwich in late July, but were defeated a few days later by government forces. Kett himself was tried for treason and hanged.

A more extensive uprising against enclosure took place in 1607. The Midland Revolt attracted considerable support in Leicestershire, Warwickshire and Northamptonshire, with matters coming to a climax in the Northants village of Newton where hedges were pulled up and ditches filled in. The Midland Revolt was also suppressed, this time by a force of local landowners and their servants. The leader of the rebels John Reynolds ('Captain Pouch'), like Robert Kett, ended his life on the gallows. The fields remained enclosed.

According to English Heritage, we know of 3,000 or so mediaeval deserted villages across the country, the number having risen significantly in recent years as more have been found (W.G. Hoskins talked of around 1,300 deserted villages having been identified when he was writing *The Making of the English Landscape* in the 1950s). Aerial photography has aided this work of research and indeed Gainsthorpe was the first deserted village to be identified from the air, back in 1925. What's to be seen at Gainsthorpe today is only part of what is believed to have been a bigger mediaeval settlement, most of the rest of it having been ploughed up over the intervening centuries, but nevertheless English Heritage still describes what's left as one of the best preserved examples. It took over the site in 1974.

What is it about deserted villages that resonates with us today? As I approached Gainsthorpe on what was a mid-week day in Autumn, I could see that I was not the village's only visitor: through the rain clouds I saw that there were already other people exploring the earthworks and making their way in among the old tofts and crofts. So why did they, and I, want to come here?

There is, I think, something we still find poignant about visiting places where, once, human beings lived out their lives. Villages like Gainsthorpe remind us perhaps that we can't count on the way things are today always necessarily being the same tomorrow. Things change, places – and people – die and human settlement of the land can evidently be a temporary thing.

I'd cycled more than four hundred miles by the time I arrived at Gainsthorpe, through an English landscape which, as I discovered, had changed over the centuries more perhaps than we imagine. I had been to towns which had developed the way they had because they were the centres of local political power. I had been to other places – like Corby – where it was economics that determined their growth. It seemed appropriate to be nearing the end of my journey at somewhere at the other end of its lifecycle, a village which had died.

Oliver Goldsmith's poem *The Deserted Village*, published in 1770 as Parliamentary enclosure was getting under way, may not be much read today but had a profound effect on readers both of his own time and later, in the nineteenth century. His poem is both a nostalgic paean to a lost pastoral idyll (the kindly priest, the firm but fair schoolmaster, the bucolic village life of the inn) and a protest at enclosure, the creation of landscaped parklands and the pursuit of wealth.

Another, later, less well-known poet also tackled the same theme, this time in a poem called *The Depopulated Village*. The author is someone we have met already – it is the nineteenth century Dorset schoolmaster William Barnes – and although Beaminster is now very many miles away and although I'm not sure that Barnes's poem is necessarily of the highest literary quality it feels somehow right if I end this chapter with an extract. It feels like coming full circle.

Barnes is this time eschewing dialect for standard English:

As oft I see by sight, or oft
In mind, the ridges on the ground,
The mark of many a little croft
And house where now no wall is found,
I call the folk to life again
And build their houses up anew…

I call them back to path or door
In warm-cheek'd life below the sun,
And see them tread their foot-worn floor
That now is all by grass o'errun….

Winteringham

For so long Winteringham had just been a name for me, a place where the pencil line I'd drawn on the pages I'd torn from my road atlas finally came to a halt. Now I had arrived.

I pedalled into Winteringham on the very last few miles of Ermine Street. The Roman road which had begun in London stopped here, by the marshy banks of the Humber estuary. This had once been the frontier of the Roman Empire, where the writ of Rome ran no further. Then, after 71 AD following the Roman advance into the northern lands beyond the Humber, Winteringham became a ferry port, the southern terminal for the crossing to Petuaria (Brough) on the north bank of the estuary.

So for over three hundred years, Winteringham was important. Excavations on the site of the Roman settlement, just to the east of the present village, have turned up a host of artefacts, things like pottery and coins and tiles and jewellery, much of it now safely deposited in Scunthorpe's town museum. Winteringham in those days would have been a worthy destination for anyone making a journey through the English countryside.

Today, it's somewhat different. Winteringham is a small village, with a church, a pub, a shop, a fancy restaurant, and a cluster of houses. There weren't many options open to me to celebrate my arrival. It was mid-afternoon, too late I felt for a lunchtime drink in the pub and certainly too early for the nine course 'surprise menu' (£85+) in the restaurant. Would the restaurant even serve soggy cyclists in waterproofs and lycra? I could have called into the shop and bought myself a flapjack or bar of chocolate, but that seemed altogether like an example of the dictionary definition of bathos.

So I continued on my bike, a short distance north from the village centre, to the edge of the Humber. Here, at Winteringham Haven, I dismounted, leaned the bike against a gate and looked out across the reeds to the water beyond. This, I felt, was the place to stop. This would be an adequate Destination.

What had I discovered on my journey to Winteringham? I'd found that a bicycle is an ideal mode of transport if you're not in a hurry and can choose the quiet roads. I'd enjoyed the way that, day by day, my bike and I had begun to work together as a team. I'd seen whole areas of England that I'd never before visited. I'd seen the landscape change. I'd seen the houses and churches built of oolite limestone stay more or less the same.

I'd had intimate encounters with roads of all kinds, some (often in the most unlikely places) with pancake-smooth tarmac surfaces, some (where highway authorities should have known better) pot-holed and set to throw me. I'd been on lanes with high banks where grass grew in the middle of the single carriageway. I'd met hills. I'd passed over the M4, the M40, the M1 and the A1. I'd crossed a solitary ford.

I had had an exceptional vantage point for researching the roadkill on England's roads. I'd seen game birds and small mammals aplenty but not a single hedgehog. I fear that what we are told is true: hedgehogs are indeed a species in rapid decline.

I had travelled through ten English counties, if you include a short dalliance with Rutland and an even shorter incursion into that part of ex-Northamptonshire which became Cambridgeshire and then Peterborough. It had been a privilege to have the time to explore my country slowly and methodically.

Had I found Middle England? I don't know. If I had, I can report that it is a place of contrast, of change, perhaps even of hope. Don't believe the stereotypes.

Eight days on the road. Burton Bradstock to Winteringham. Except that I couldn't stop in Winteringham. I picked up the bike where I'd put it by the reed-beds, swung my leg over the pannier bags and the rear wheel and headed back the way I had come, back to the village centre. There were three trains to catch to get me safely home. I turned south and made for Scunthorpe station.

Acknowledgements and references

This book is, I hope, about more than a bike ride. But I did cycle from Burton Bradstock to Winteringham over eight days in September 2016 and I need first to thank those who helped make the trip possible.

I cycled by myself from Witney to Kettering, and from Stamford north through Sleaford and Lincoln to the Humber. For the first three days, however, I enjoyed the company of two friends, Peter McCarthy and Chris Green, who came along to see me safely on my way. I am very grateful for the way they helped me up those steep Dorset and Cotswold hills and made the whole experience so special.

It was a pleasure too to cycle from Kettering to Stamford with my old friend from university days Paul Ticher, and I have to thank Paul and his partner Gill Taylor for cooking me a meal and putting me up in their home at the end of my sixth day of travelling. Thanks too go to my cycling and running friends at home for their encouragement, particularly to Phil Hodgson who lent me panniers and a handlebar bag and who gave me all sorts of tips for what to do/not do. Kate Ashbrook offered helpful comments on the draft text. A particular thank you to Jane Scullion, for transporting me and my bicycle to Dorset in the first instance and for so much else besides.

You will gather that many people generously gave me their time, agreeing to answer my perhaps sometimes naive questions. Most of these interviews necessarily had to be done at a separate time from the bike ride (sweaty cyclists are not in the best position to undertake in-depth interviews), and mostly were undertaken a few weeks later. But I was strict with myself when planning this book: I made sure that I only interviewed people who were very close to the actual route I had cycled. My grateful thanks to: Malcolm Turnbull, Denys Brunsden, Vanessa White, Brendon Owen, Peter Macfadyen, Alex Robertson, Verona Bass, Colin Tudge, Ruth West, Geoff Tansey, David Chambers, Julian Palmer, Robin and Kate Shaw, John Hoy, Peter Couchman, Jacqui Norton, Tom Beattie, Sandra and Paul Johnson, Chris Gardiner, James Truscott, Peter Roberts, Paul Booth.

I have chosen not to clutter the text with footnotes, but I don't want to fall into the trap of those travel books that make assertions without stating their sources. Since I certainly haven't been afraid to make assertions, what follows is an account of the main sources I have used.

Introduction, Burton Bradstock

W.G. Hoskins, *The Making of the English Landscape*, Hodder & Stoughton, 1955.

The standard introduction to William Smith is Simon Winchester's book *The Map that Changed the World*, Viking, 2001.

The documents for the UNESCO World Heritage bid are still available, on the UNESCO website: http://whc.unesco.org/en/list/1029/documents/. The website for the Jurassic Coast itself is http://jurassiccoast.org and the British Geological Survey online maps are at http://mapapps.bgs.ac.uk/geologyofbritain/home.html.

I also used:

Richard Fortey, *The Hidden Landscape*, Bodley Head, 2010.

British Geological Survey, *Bedrock Geology UK South*, BGS, 2008.

W.J. Arkell, *The Jurassic System in Great Britain*, Oxford: Clarendon, 1933.

Powerstock

William Barnes' poetry is available in several editions. I used the selection edited by Chris Wrigley (Dovecote Press, 1984).

On West Country dialect:

Peter Trudgill, *The Dialects of England*, Blackwell, 1990.

Powerstock and District Community Land Trust's website is www.pdclt.co.uk. The national website for the CLT network is http://www.communitylandtrusts.org.uk/.

Odcombe

Stephen Price in 1870 produced an account of George Mitchell's life, including a section of Mitchell's own writings. This book, with the lengthy title *The Skeleton at the Plough, or, The poor farm labourers of the west: with the autobiography and reminiscences of George Mitchell "one from the plough"* has been digitised and can be found at https://archive.org/details/perkins59571432.

More recently Brendon Owen from Montacute village has produced his own biography: *One From the Plough, The life and times of George Mitchell 1826-1901* (Gazebo Press, 2001).

Francis George Heath's books with relevance to the Montacute story are *'Romance' of Peasant Life* (Cassell, Petter and Galpin, 1872) and *The English Peasantry* (Frederick Warne, 1874).

Roy Palmer was an inspirational teacher and author whose anthologies of industrial and agricultural ballads (although purportedly written as educational books) are a delight. The song I quote is included by Palmer in *The Painful Plough: a portrait of the agricultural labourer in the nineteenth century from folk songs and ballads and contemporary accounts* (Cambridge University Press, 1973). I also recommend Roy Palmer's *The Sound of History: Songs and Social Comment* (Oxford University Press, 1988).

For an account of attempts at agricultural trade unions: Reg Groves, *Sharpen the Sickle*, Porcupine Press, 1949. For an academic study of Hodge: Mark Freeman, "The agricultural labourer and the 'Hodge' stereotype, c 1850-1914", in *Agricultural History Review*, 49, II, pp172-186. For the classic history of the Captain Swing uprisings: Eric Hobsbawm and George Rudé, *Captain Swing,* Lawrence & Wishart 1969.

T.S. Eliot's *Four Quartets* can be found in his collected works. The Local Plan for Yeovil and surrounding areas is available at https://www.southsomerset.gov.uk.

Frome

Peter Macfadyen's book is *Flatpack Democracy* (eco-logic books, 2014).
I used the selection of William Cobbett's *Rural Rides* published by Penguin in 1967. The text is also digitised online, https://archive.org/stream/ruralrides01cobb/ruralrides01cobb_djvu.txt.

Bathampton

Data on UK agriculture used in this chapter come from various sources:
Defra/National Statistics, *Agriculture in the United Kingdom 2015,* 2016, https://www.gov.uk/government/statistics/agriculture-in-the-united-kingdom-2015. [data on average farm sizes, employment in agriculture, age of farmers]
Eurostat, Farm structure survey 2014, http://ec.europa.eu/eurostat [European farm sizes]
Defra/National Statistics, *Farm Household Income and Household Composition 2014/15,* 2016. [household composition in agriculture]
The Landworkers' Alliance and The Land magazine, *Equality in the Countryside, A Rural Manifesto,* 2016. [food self-sufficiency, data on large landownership]
The Landworkers' Alliance and The Land magazine, *More Farmers – Better Food,* 2015. [food self-sufficiency]
New Economics Foundation, *Urgent Recall,* 2014. [farm size, CAP subsidies, employment in agriculture]
Oxford Farming Conference, *Power in Agriculture – a Vital Report on the Future of Farming,* 2012. [international trade in fertilisers]
Colin Tudge, *Six steps back to the land,* Green Books, 2016.
The Dry Arch Growers website is https://bathamptoncsa.wordpress.com.
The national Community Supported Agriculture site is
http://www.communitysupportedagriculture.org.uk.
Websites linked to Colin Tudge's work include:
http://www.campaignforrealfarming.org, http://www.feanetwork.org,
http://www.orfc.org.uk

Cirencester, Salperton

Thomas Hobbes's *Leviathan* is available in many editions. I used the 2014 edition from Wordsworth, with an introduction by Richard Serjeantson.

My reference to local protests at housing plans from the Bathurst estate comes from the Cirencester Scene magazine (late 2016). The article on shooting at Salperton can be found at https://www.fieldsportsmagazine.com.

On Cotswold new towns, burgage plots and such things I found The Friends of the Cotswolds's *Northleach Historic Town walking trail* interesting.

Naunton

Two websites: http://www.churchillheritage.org.uk;
http://www.cotswoldstonequarries.co.uk.

Adlestrop

The collected poems of Edward Thomas have been edited by R. George Thomas, (Oxford University Press, 1981).
 There are two recent biographies:
Matthew Hollis, *Now all roads lead to France: the last years of Edward Thomas*, Windsor, 2012.
Jean Moorcroft Wilson, *Edward Thomas: from Adlestrop to Arras: a biography*, Bloomsbury, 2015.
 Thomas's prose works include *The Heart of England* (Dent, 1906) *South Country* (Dent, 1909), *In Pursuit of Spring* (Nelson, 1914; new edition Little Toller Books, 2016). *One Green Field* (Penguin, 2009) is an anthology of prose works from Thomas.
 My quote on Thomas towards the end of this chapter comes from the essay by H. Coombes "Hardy, de la Mare and Edward Thomas" in *The Pelican Guide to English Literature 7*, Penguin, 1961.

Charterville

Alice Mary Hadfield's *The Chartist Land Company* (David & Charles, 1970) while including the Charterville story is not quite the definitive history one would wish for.
 I've also used:
Paul A. Pickering, *Feargus O'Connor*, Merlin Press, 2008.
Dennis Hardy, *Alternative Communities in Nineteenth Century England*, Longman, 1979.
Malcolm Chase, *The People's Farm, English Radical Agrarianism 1775-1840*, Oxford University Press, 1988 (reprinted Breviary Stuff 2010).
Malcolm Chase, *The Chartists, Perspectives and legacies*, Merlin Press, 2015.
C.W. Stubbs, *The Land and the Labourers*, Swan Sonnenschein and Co, 1885.
Arthur W. Ashby, *Allotments and Small Holdings in Oxfordshire*, Oxford: Clarendon, 1917.
Joy MacAskill, "The Chartist Land Plan", in Asa Briggs (ed), *Chartist Studies*, Macmillan 1959.
Kate Tiller, "Charterville and the Chartist Land Company", in *Oxoniensia*, L (1985).
 Information on the Rosedene Chartist cottage is at https://www.nationaltrust.org.uk/rosedene.

Blenheim

The Blenheim Palace website is http://www.blenheimpalace.com/. For shooting at Blenheim see https://www.iancoley.co.uk/blenheim-palace-shooting/.

On land values:

DCLG, *Land value estimates for policy appraisal,* Dec 2015

Valuation Office Agency, *Property Market Report,* 2011

Steeple Barton

As mentioned above, *The Making of the English Landscape* was first published in 1955.

I also used:

Maurice Beresford, "Professor WG Hoskins – a Memoir" in *British Agricultural History,* 1992.

Matthew H. Johnson, "On the Particularism of English Landscape Archaeology" in *International Journal of Historical Archaeology,* Vol.9, No. 2, June 2005.

Juniper Hill

Lark Rise was first published in 1939, and the combined volume *Lark Rise to Candleford* came out in 1945 (Oxford University Press).

Helmdon

My information on the Great Central Railway is taken from:

Michael J. Soar, *The New Line to London of the Great Central Railway: Centenary Edition 1899-1999,* published 1999.

Wellingborough

Two websites: http://www.diggersfestival.org.uk; http://www.rogerlovejoy.co.uk/philosophy/diggers/diggers3.htm.

For Gerrard Winstanley's writings, I used the1973 Penguin edition *The Law of Freedom and Other Writings.*

Other books used on the Diggers:

Christopher Hill, *The World Turned Upside Down,* Maurice Temple Smith, 1972.

John Gurney, *Brave Community,* Manchester University Press, 2007.

John Gurney, *Gerrard Winstanley,* Pluto Press, 2013.

Andrew Bradstock (ed), *Winstanley and the Diggers 1649-1999,* Frank Cass, 2000.

Tony Benn, *Gerrard Winstanley a Common Treasury,* Verso, London, 2011.

I'm grateful for Jacqui Norton for drawing my attention to this (anonymous) article:

"Diggers at Wellingborough", in *The Northampton County Magazine,* Vol. 5, January 1932.

Two other books mentioned in this chapter:

Andro Linklater, *Owning the Earth,* Bloomsbury, 2014.

Kevin Cahill, *Who Owns Britain,* Canongate, 2001.

My thanks to Leon Rosselson for granting permission to reproduce the lines from his song *The World Turned Upside Down.*

Corby

Ebenezer Howard's *To-morrow, A Peaceful Path to Real Reform* (1898) is better known under the name used for the second edition *Garden Cities of To-morrow* (Swan Sonnenschein, 1902).
Colin Ward's *New Town, Home Town* (Calouste Gulbenkian, 1993) is a fascinating look at the post-war new town experience.
The Apethorpe press release mentioned: http://www.english-heritage.org.uk/visit/places/apethorpe-palace/future-secured/.

Collyweston

Two websites: http://www.plunkett.co.uk; https://collywestonshop.co.uk.
    Stamford library has an interesting archive box of material on the Collyweston slate industry, including the anonymous *Collyweston Stone Slates* (u.d.). An interview with a retired miner Claude Smith was published in the Rutland and Stamford Mercury, March 23 2012.

Barnack

Information on the Fens Waterways Link can be found at various websites including https://www.waterways.org.uk and https://ousewasheslps.wordpress.com/2013/08/15/the-fens-waterways-link/.
    Information on the Hills and Holes nature reserve: http://publications.naturalengland.org.uk/publication/4529218465562624; http://fbhh.org.uk/.
    For the Wildlife Trusts website: http://www.wildlifetrusts.org/. For Burghley House: http://www.burghley.co.uk/.
    Two other books:
Raymond Williams, *The Country and the City*, Chatto and Windus 1973.
Raymond Williams, *Politics and Letters*, Verso, 1981.

Helpston

I used the Oxford University Press edition of John Clare's selected poetry and prose, edited by Eric Robinson and Geoffrey Summerfield (1966).
    I would recommend John Barrell's 1972 book *The Idea of Landscape and the Sense of Place 1730-1840, an approach to the poetry of John Clare* (Cambridge University Press).
    On commons, commoners' rights and enclosures:
J.M. Neeson, *Commoners: Common Right, Enclosure and Social Change in England, 1700-1820*, (Cambridge University Press, 1993).
E.P. Thompson, *Customs in Common* (particularly Chapter III), Merlin Press, 1991.
    I also used:
Briony McDonagh and Stephen Daniels, "Enclosure stories: narratives from Northamptonshire" in *Cultural Geographies* 19.1 (2012).
John Felstiner, "Its only Bondage was the Circling Sky: John Clare and the Enclosure of Helpston", in *The Land* 8, Winter 2009/10.
John Goodridge, "Pastoral and popular modes in Clare's 'enclosure elegies'" available online from http://www.johnclare.info.

Sleaford

Websites:
http://www.nationalcraftanddesign.org.uk/
https://acorp.uk.com/
   On poaching and the Black Act:
E.P. Thompson, *Whigs and Hunters*, Allen Lane, 1975.

Branston

Websites: http://www.branston.com/;
https://potatoes.ahdb.org.uk/;
http://www.lincsfoodandfarming.org.uk/;
https://www.lincolnshire.gov.uk/residents/environment-and-planning/
environment/environmental-report/part-c-land/agriculture/100437.article.
   Other resources used:
Improve Food and Drink Skills Council, *Skills Needs in the Greater Lincolnshire Agri-food Sector*, 2012.
Greater Lincolnshire Local Enterprise Partnership, *Strategic Economic Plan*, 2013.
Defra/National Statistics, *Agriculture in the United Kingdom 2015*, 2016. (And see also other resources listed above, under Bathampton).
   On the Huguenots in Lincolnshire:
Trevor Bevis, *The River Makers*, published by the author, 1999.

Lincoln

Website: https://lincolncathedral.com/.

Gainsthorpe

Information about Gainsthorpe deserted mediaeval village can be found at both the English Heritage website (http://www.english-heritage.org.uk) and the Pastscape website (http://www.pastscape.org.uk).
   For mediaeval enclosure history, I used various sources already referenced, including W.G. Hoskins and Raymond Williams. I also used the essay by Simon Fairlie "A Short History of Enclosure in Britain" in *The Land*, 7, Summer 2009, and also available online.
   My edition of Sir Thomas More's *Utopia* is the Wordsworth edition (1997), with an introduction by Mishtooni Bose. The translation is by Ralph Robinson (1556) with modernised spelling.

Winteringham

For information on the archaeology and Roman remains, I used the http://www.pastscape.org.uk website. There are interpretation boards at Winteringham Haven, put up as part of the South Humber Heritage Trail.

Index